Granny Quilt Décor

Darlene Zimmerman

©2004 by Darlene Zimmerman
Published by

krause publications
An F+W Publications Company

700 East State Street • Iola, WI 54990-0001
715-445-2214 • 888-457-2873
www.krause.com

Our toll-free number to place an order or obtain a free catalog is 800-258-0929.

Library of Congress Catalog Number: 2003116740

ISBN: 0-87349-758-9

Edited by Nicole Gould
Designed by Sharon Laufenberg

Printed in China

Acknowledgments

I would like to thank the following people for their help, encouragement, and expertise:

■ My family for their continued support and encouragement.

■ My daughter, Rachel, for her hard work on the designs and illustrations.

■ Pam Kienholz for her expert hand-quilting and help above and beyond the call of duty!

■ Margy Manderfeld for sharing her "Perfect Fit" binding technique, her friendship, and her helpful advice.

■ All my quilting friends for their enthusiasm!

■ Julie Stephani and the staff at Krause for their friendship and efforts.

■ The design department at EZ Quilting for providing the graphics for the tool tutorial.

■ Chanteclaire Fabrics, Inc. for providing fabrics; A&E Thread Co. for providing thread; and Fairfield Corp. for supplying batting.

■ Special thanks to the Colonial Pattern Co. for allowing me to use their cherry design in several of the projects.

■ The anonymous makers of the vintage quilts displayed in this book.

■ My editor, Niki Gould, for her expertise, enthusiasm, and all her hard work!

Table of Contents

The Bedroom

The Child's Room

The Nursery

Introduction

In the fall of 2002, when the first Granny Quilts book was published, I knew there would be another Granny book to follow. I had so many ideas and too many wonderful vintage quilt tops in my collection to stop with just one '30s book! Quilts from this era are so pretty and appealing that I wanted to stretch the boundaries a bit further and incorporate the '30s look into not only full-size quilts, but also pillows, table runners, and wall hangings. The projects are all shown in room settings to help you to integrate the "'30s look" into your decorating scheme.

Quilts from the '30s era are enjoying a renewed popularity. These lovely pastel quilts, often made with sewing scraps or feedsacks during the hard times of the war years and the Great Depression, continue to tug at our heartstrings. For some of us, these are the quilts we grew up with—the quilts our grandmas, aunts, or mothers made. So, naturally, those quilts have sentimental value. However, the soft colors, the infinite variety of the patches, and the familiar patterns appeal to our artistic side as well.

These '30s quilts (new or vintage) are perfect to use in the new lighter, brighter color schemes in our homes today. They mix equally well with antiques or contemporary furniture. They're perfect with any garden-themed room and are lovely in a bedroom for a child of any age! If you aren't lucky enough to own a vintage beauty, then this book will help you create special heirlooms for yourself or your loved ones.

History

To understand what makes these quilts from the '30s era so appealing, we need to go back in time. Quilts from the early and mid-1800s looked much different. The colors were usually dark and somber, and the range of color was limited. People wore dark-colored clothing, and their quilts were usually made from their sewing and clothing scraps. Standards of cleanliness were not what they are now. Their severely limited wardrobes and the custom of taking a bath on Saturday night only (whether one needed it or not!) made dark clothing more practical.

Also, at this earlier time, all dyes were natural (vegetable based), and were prone to fading and bleeding. Quilters, of course, wanted to use the most colorfast fabrics, which explains the popularity of particular hues: indigos (various shades of blue), Turkey red (so named because of the long and involved dye process actually developed in the country of Turkey), chrome-yellow (safety yellow), antimony orange, double-pinks (pink prints on pink backgrounds), browns and blacks, and madder reds and oranges. Green was a difficult color to dye; it was obtained by dyeing yellow over blue or blue over yellow. The brown/black prints were often dyed with manganese and iron, which damaged the fabric. So, in many old quilts you see the browns and blacks have rotted away, bled, or faded.

Favorite color schemes of quilters in the mid-1800s were red and green on a white background for appliqué or "best" quilts, brown and double pink, or indigo blue and white. You will see quite a bit of brown in quilts from this era, not necessarily because they used brown prints frequently, but because many other colors have faded to a soft brown, notably purple and black prints.

Near the end of the 1800s and into the early 1900s, quilts began to incorporate shirting fabrics (tiny black or dark blue designs on white backgrounds), mourning gray prints (finely detailed black prints on white backgrounds that appear to be gray prints), and burgundy (instead of Turkey red); indigo (dark blue) prints continued to be popular. Quilts from this era often have a "patriotic" look to them.

For a time around the turn of the century, traditional quilts "went out of style." Crazy quilts were all the rage, touted by women's magazines that looked down on the "old-fashioned patch quilt." Crazy quilts were usually made up of silks, satins, and velvets in irregular shapes placed upon a foundation. Often souvenir ribbons and mementos of important events were incorporated, along with names and dates. They were heavily embroidered and were intended to be used in the Victorian parlors. Crazy quilts were a statement of wealth, showing you had the time and the money to waste making a useless quilt. Old-time quilt makers said, "If you weren't crazy when you started one, you were crazy when you finished one!"

Redwork and bluework were also popular around the turn of the century. Stamped squares ("penny squares") could be bought for a penny at the local store and were then embroidered with either Turkey red or dark blue floss. Many a young girl learned to embroider on penny squares. It's interesting to note that redwork has become popular once again.

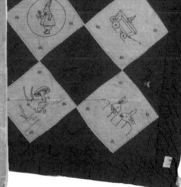

This penny squares crib quilt was found inside of a tied comforter.

Up until WWI, Germany had been the leader in producing dyes for fabric. While we were at war with Germany, new dyes had to be developed, and these new dyes came from petroleum products. Now new colorfast pastel colors were available: butter yellow, lavender, "that" green, pink, sky blue, tangerine (orange), peach, and red. These "new" pastel fabrics were inexpensive and widely available. The government even promoted quiltmaking with the slogan "Make quilts; save the blankets for the boys over there," while newspapers, women's magazines, and department stores all promoted quilting and provided quilting patterns and kits. New patterns that have become synonymous with that era appeared: Double Wedding Ring, Dresden Plate, Grandmother's Flower Garden, and Sunbonnet Sue.

The quilts from the '30s era shared many common "threads": a wide variety of prints and/or solids, many times from dressmaking scraps; a pastel color scheme; and interesting border treatments. Nearly every housewife sewed her own and her family's clothing, as well as aprons, curtains, pillows, and other decorative items. Most, if not all, clothing was sewn from cotton fabric, and the scraps were used for making quilts. The patterns mentioned earlier were ideal for using up small pieces of fabric. Women prided themselves on their frugality, so quiltmaking became a natural extension of their sewing skills.

Quilts made with soft pastels are generally lumped together under the name "'30s quilts", denoting a time span from approximately 1920 to 1950. Within that era there are some subtle differences. Earlier fabrics and quilts from that time period show a predominance of soft pastels in small-scale prints. As we move to the end of the era, the colors become brighter and the scale of the patterns becomes larger and bolder. Of course, this is just a rough estimate of age. Quilts were usually made using sewing scraps—and the scrap bag may have held fabrics that spanned a period of 50 years! Quilt historians 100 years from now will have a difficult task indeed; today we use both vintage and reproduction fabrics from all eras in our quilts. Without documentation (do make sure to sign and date your quilts!), their task will be impossible.

Feedsacks, those colorful cloth bags that originally held anything from flour and sugar to chicken feed, played an important role in our society as well as in quiltmaking. Before the advent of plastic bags and cardboard boxes, foodstuffs were packaged in kegs or barrels until the mid-1800s. After that time, cloth bags of various sizes were used. Until the late 1920s, these bags were usually white, brown, or other solid colors. Naturally the frugal housewife would recycle these—bleach out the logo and put them to use as household linens, clothing, and quilt pieces.

Sometime in the late 1920s, bag manufacturers began to print designs on the bags. Even those housewives that did not live on a farm had a steady supply of these bags coming into their homes. Most women baked their own bread, and the flour, sugar, cornmeal, and other dry goods came packaged in these printed cloth bags. Many farmwomen raised chickens to sell or for egg money, and they had a larger supply of printed feedsacks, or "chicken linen," as the sacks were sometimes called. The large bags (50#) measure about 36" x 45" (a yard of fabric in today's measurements); the smaller bags are about half that size. The feedsacks can be readily identified by size (36" wide) and by the telltale holes running along the selvage made by the string as the bags were sewn together.

Feedsacks were so widely used, it's a wonder that any survive today! But, we have to remember that they were printed in huge quantities over a 30-year time span. In 1942 alone, about 50 million feedsacks were manufactured and sold. In that same year, one plant alone was printing 1,000 different designs. Nearly everyone in this country at one time was wearing clothing made from feedsacks. It was virtually indistinguishable from fabric purchased off the bolt, and it was free! Naturally, feedsack fabric found it's way into quilts, but unless you find those tell-tale holes on a patch, you can never be sure if it's feedsack fabric or not.

For many people, feedsacks trigger fond memories of growing up and wearing clothing made of them. Here are a few stories:

"I remember going with my father to "help" him pick out the sacks of chicken feed…"
— Grace McMullen, NY

"I remember making curtains for my bedroom out of feedsack fabric in the 50's."
— Cynthia Erickson, MN

"When I was a little girl, my father raced pigeons. He always bought feed for them in the big sacks. We had so much of that material and my mother threw it all away years ago. Just seeing it brings back pleasant memories."
— Susan Leary, MD

"I grew up wearing dresses my mother made from feedsacks. She talks about how important it was for my father to get the right print if she was not with him, so she would be sure to have enough of the same one to complete her sewing project."
— Portia Figland, IA

"I grew up with my mom making my school costumes out of feedsacks, as my dad was a cattle rancher. Feedsacks used to be so colorful!"
— Betty Florentz, TX

"I wore feedsack print dresses and skirts as a child and a teenager!"
— Mary Ann Mikesell, FL

"The feedsacks remind me so much of my grandmother and all the things she used to make with them."
— Pam Wenzel, TX

"My grandmother made all my clothes from feedsacks as a child and taught me to quilt and love sewing!"
— Melinda Gasparik, VA

"We had chickens in our back yard (and a chicken coop) when I was growing up. My mother made many of my clothes from feedsacks."
— Mary Ernwine, KY

"When I was in high school, my mother encouraged me to enter a contest at the Tennessee State Fair. You had to make a garment out of cotton feedsacks. My grandmother gave me enough to make a shirtwaist dress, sleeveless with a straight skirt. The sacks had a white background and little red roses. I won first place at the State Fair and my garment was sent on to the Cotton Carnival to compete in Memphis. I won first place and won the first sewing machine of my very own."
— Ila C. Long, TN

General Instructions

Choosing Fabric

Quilts with the "'30s look" are some of the easiest to make. We are so fortunate to have so many great reproduction fabrics available to us today. The projects in this book call for a variety of prints—usually more is better. Since most of them are medium tones, you need only think of having a good mix of color—and the colors will all work together. It's okay to put red with pink and green with blue; they will work together. And, I urge you to use a few of the darker prints—red, dark blues, dark yellow. They add a note of interest and "spark" up the pastels when sprinkled liberally across the quilt top.

Background fabric in quilts from this era was usually plain white, but sometimes a solid color was used instead. I like to use Vintage White from Chanteclaire, as it's a mellow shade of white, not bright white.

The fabric you choose should be good quality, 100% cotton. If you choose to pre-wash, pre-wash ALL the fabric. Or, you can pre-test your fabric for bleeding by spritzing it with water and ironing it dry over a square of white cotton. If you have color transference onto the white square, then be sure to pre-wash.

Cutting

In each of the patterns in this book, all the larger pieces of fabric are cut selvage to selvage, unless noted otherwise. After the strips are cut, the To Yield column will tell you the number of pieces to cut from these strips, and which tool to use. **The tools are not interchangeable.** If you choose not to use the tools listed, alternate cutting directions are given or templates are provided.

A Tool Tutorial is given on pages 125 to 127. Familiarize yourself with the tools before using them in a project. While all of them are easy to use, they must be used correctly for best results.

Take the time to cut the strips and pieces accurately, as this will mean fewer problems when piecing later. Never cut more than two layers at a time. Any time saved in cutting more layers will be lost in struggling to get the pieces to fit together.

Sewing

Quarter-inch seams are used throughout. It is **very important** to sew exact ¼" seams. Most sewing machines have ¼" feet available and are well worth the small investment.

 Try this quick test to see if you are sewing an exact 1/4" seam:

Cut three 1½" x 3½" strips. Sew them together on the long edges. Press. The square should measure exactly 3½". If not, adjust your seam allowance and/or pressing technique.

The sizes for the unfinished blocks and units are given in the patterns. This is to keep you on track. That said, however, it is more important for your blocks to be the same size rather than the exact size given in the pattern.

Pressing

Proper pressing is so important! Follow the pressing arrows given in the instructions. Or, if no pressing directions are given, press the seam in the way it wants to fall. Remember to press **flat**; do not pull up on a corner and inadvertently tug out of square while pressing.

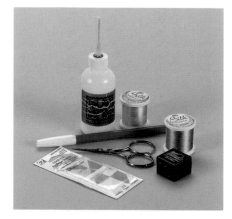

Appliqué Techniques

Below are two different appliqué techniques. You may choose either one or use your favorite method.

Freezer Paper Appliqué

Step 1. The patterns given in the book (starting on page 118) are reversed unless they are the same either way (butterfly, leaf). Trace the shapes on the dull side of freezer paper.

> **Note:** *You can re-use the freezer paper patterns several times.*

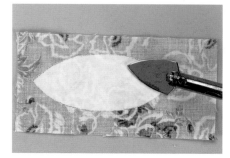

Step 2. Cut out the shapes on the lines. Iron to the wrong side of the fabrics chosen, leaving at least ¾" between the shapes. Cut out the shapes adding a scant ¼" seam allowance. Clip any inside corners.

Step 3. With a 1:1 liquid spray starch and water mixture (or light spray starch), spray the fabric side of the appliqué pieces. Using the tip of the iron, or the tiny iron, press the seam allowances over the edge of the freezer paper. Once the edge is well pressed, you can remove the freezer paper and iron on the top side.

Step 4. Use the pattern (or the illustration given with the project) and trace it onto the background square with the blue washout marker. Using Roxanne's Glue-Baste It™ or basting thread, position and baste the shape in place on your background fabric.

Step 5. Appliqué down by hand with matching thread or use a tiny zigzag stitch on your sewing machine. Another option would be to use a buttonhole stitch and black thread (machine) or floss (hand). For hand appliqué, silk thread in a light cream color works with most fabrics. The thread "melts" into the fabric, making your stitches nearly invisible.

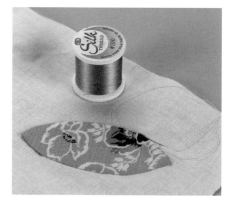

> **Tip:** *Using Thread Heaven—similar to beeswax—on the silk thread prevents it from tangling.*

Fusible Appliqué

Step 1. The patterns in the back of the book are reversed for tracing unless they are the same either way (butterfly, leaf). Trace onto the paper side of the fusible web, leaving a bit of space between each.

Step 2. Roughly cut out each shape and iron to the wrong side of the fabric chosen for the appliqué. Note that on large pieces you only need to fuse the edges, so cut the center out of the shape. Follow the manufacturer's directions for fusing.

Step 3. Cut out on the drawn line. Fuse in place, layering as necessary. If this project will be washed and used, the edges of the appliqué should be stitched down with matching or invisible thread, using a tiny zigzag, blind hem, or buttonhole stitch.

Making Four-Patches

Use this little trick to help reduce the bulk and keep those four-patch seams lying flat.

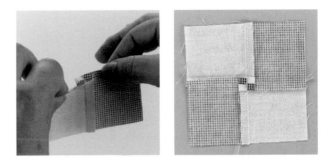

Step 1. Before pressing the last seam in a four-patch, grasp the seam with both hands about an inch from the center seam. Twist in opposite directions, opening up a few threads in the seam.

Step 2. Press one seam down and the other seam up, and in the center you will see a tiny four-patch appear. The center will now lie flatter without the bother of pressing the seams open.

Embroidery Stitches

Several of the projects in this book call for embroidery stitches.

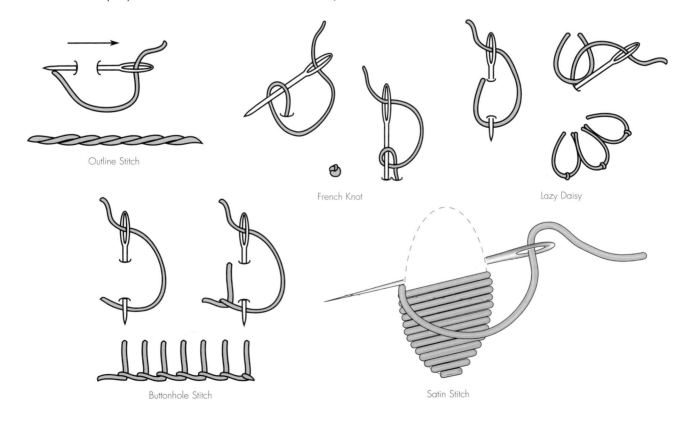

Outline Stitch

French Knot

Lazy Daisy

Buttonhole Stitch

Satin Stitch

Adding Borders

Borders are the frame for your quilt and should enhance the quilt. Feel free to change the fabric selections and/or border width on any of the patterns.

 Note: *In some of the patterns, the borders are cut lengthwise to avoid having to piece the wide outer borders. This is indicated in the length of strips to cut.*

Step 1. Prepare the borders by cutting the number of strips required and piecing them together, either on the diagonal or straight of grain, whichever is less noticeable. Press the seams open.

Step 2. Measure the width of the quilt top. A painless way of determining the proper length to cut your borders is to simply use the borders to "measure" the width of the quilt. Layer the top and bottom border strips aligned with the left edge of your quilt (away from the top edge, as that may have stretched), and smooth out the borders across the width of the quilt. Fold and crease the borders at the right edge of the quilt, but cut them 1" longer for "insurance."

Step 3. Match and pin the centers of the border strips and quilt top. Pin the borders to the quilt and stitch. Press, then trim off excess length.

Step 4. Repeat for the sides of the quilt.

Mitered Corners

Step 1. Measure and cut borders the width (or length) of the quilt plus border width times two, plus several more inches for insurance. Example: 52" width + 6" border + 6" border + 4" insurance = 68"

Step 2. Sew all four borders to the quilt top, centering the borders (see Step 3 above) and stitching up to ¼" from the corners. Stop and backstitch. Press the seam allowances toward the quilt.

Step 3. Fold the quilt on the diagonal, right sides together, matching raw edges, and having the excess borders extending outward.

Step 4. Lay the Companion Angle (or a ruler) on your quilt with the longest edge on the diagonal fold, and the side of the tool aligned with the raw edges of the borders. Draw a line from the diagonal fold to the edge of the borders.

Step 5. Pin the borders together along this line. Stitch on the line, backstitching at the inside corner.

Step 6. Check the seam on the right side. If it is properly sewn, trim the seam allowance to ¼" and press open. Repeat on all four corners.

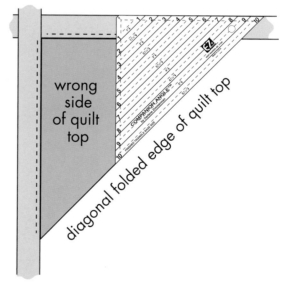

The Quilt Sandwich

When the quilt top is completed, it is time to consider the quilting. Quilting suggestions are given for each project, but feel free to choose your own method of quilting.

Some tops need to be marked for quilting before they are basted, others while they are being quilted. Whichever marking device you use, pretest it on scraps of fabric from the project to see if it can be easily removed.

Step 1. Cut batting and backing at least 4" larger than the quilt top. Thin cotton batting will give a more traditional look, but cotton batting can be a bit more difficult to hand quilt.

Step 2. Baste the three layers together with safety pins or thread 4" apart. I recommend turning the backing over the batting and top, and baste or pin in place. This prevents the edges from raveling out.

Binding

Step 1. When the quilting is completed, machine baste (with a walking foot) or hand baste a scant ¼" from the edge of the quilt. This will prevent the layers from shifting while the binding is sewn on.

Step 2. Cut the binding strips 2¼" wide for double binding, 1¼"wide for single binding. You can use either bias or straight-of-grain binding for straight edges, but you **must** use bias for curved edges. To cut bias strips, align the 45-degree line on your long ruler with the selvage and cut diagonal strips.

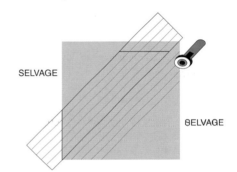

SELVAGE

SELVAGE

Step 3. Join the binding strips with diagonal seams pressed open. For a double binding, press the binding in half, wrong sides together.

Step 4. Sew the binding to the quilt with a ¼" seam, mitering the corners. To miter, sew within a seam allowance from the corner. Stop and backstitch. Remove the quilt from under the presser foot and clip threads.

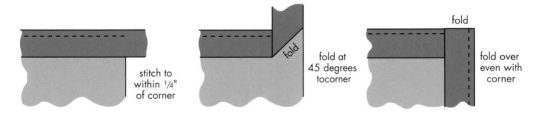

stitch to within ¼" of corner

fold

fold at 45 degrees tocorner

fold

fold over even with corner

Step 5. Fold the binding straight up, then fold it back down at the edge of the quilt, aligning the binding with the next edge of the quilt. Begin stitching at the fold. Repeat in this manner around the quilt.

"Perfect Fit" Join

Step 1. Begin stitching the binding at the middle of one of the sides of the quilt, leaving an 8" tail. Continue stitching the binding until you are within 10" of the beginning. Remove the quilt from under the needle.

Step 2. On a flat surface, pull the binding ends together to meet in the middle of that 10" space. Crease both ends where they meet, but leaving a ¼" space between the ends. Cut off one end at the crease, and the other end a binding's width from the crease. (If a double binding, open it up.)

Step 3. Join the two ends with a diagonal seam pressed open.

Step 4. Finish sewing the binding to the quilt.

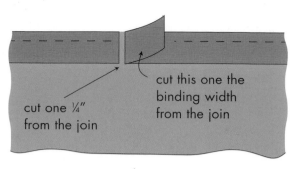

cut one ¼" from the join

cut this one the binding width from the join

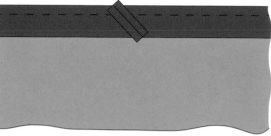

Quilt Labels

Don't forget to put a label on your quilt when it is finished. This is your legacy! A label can be as simple as signing and dating the front or back of the quilt. Artists always sign their works on the front!. Or, it can be elaborate, complete with pictures of the maker and the recipient. It could include the following information:

> Quilt recipient
> Quilt maker and quilter
> Date of completion/presentation
> Where it was made (city, country)
> Special occasion

The label can be a purchased one or a simple square of muslin with pertinent information written on it. Sew or appliqué to the front or back of your quilt after it's completed or sew to the backing before the quilt is layered.

Washing and Storing a Quilt

With reasonable care, a quilt can last for a very long time. Remember to keep it out of direct sunlight, protect it from pets and small children, and avoid high heat or humidity.

Store in a pillowcase, never in plastic which can trap moisture and bugs, or on paper or wood. Unfold and re-fold differently several times a year to prevent permanent creases from forming.

To remove the blue marks from the blue wash-out pen, **soak in cold water only,** no detergent! If a quilt needs to be washed, do so with a gentle detergent made just for this purpose. Dissolve the detergent in lukewarm water in the wash machine. Add the quilt and agitate only by hand. Let soak for a few hours. If heavily soiled or stained, soak in Oxy-clean® for up to three days. Spin to remove water. Rinse in the same manner.

To dry the quilt, lay it flat with a fan blowing over it. Turn it over when one side is dry. Wait until it is thoroughly dry before folding or storing.

With loving care, your quilts will become treasured heirlooms for generations to come.

The Front Porch

Fan-cy Dancing Quilt

Size shown: (60" x 75"), 8" finished block; queen-size: (91" x 91")
Reproduction fabrics sewn by author, machine-quilted by Bonnie Erickson.

Fan blocks are interesting because they are asymmetrical. Just like Log Cabin blocks, you can arrange them in many different ways to produce a fascinating array of designs. This quilt may look difficult, but it is very easy. There are two fans per block, set in opposite corners, and it's only the arrangement of the fans in a simple block-to-block setting that gives the quilt the appearance of being set on the diagonal.

The fan tips don't need to be appliquéd down. I simply baste the fans in place on the block, and the quilting holds them in place on the background. Using my easy technique for making those points, you can leave the tips free for a three-dimensional look. Or, if you prefer, you can hand or machine appliqué them down with an invisible stitch or use black thread and a buttonhole stitch.

Directions for a queen-size quilt are included (in parentheses).

Fabric Requirements

▶ Yellow solid: 4⅓ yd. (7¾ yd.)
▶ Dark blue solid: 1⅔ yd. (2½ yd.)
▶ Variety of prints: 10(21) fat quarters

Suggested Tools and Supplies

▶ Easy Dresden™
▶ Bamboo point turner
▶ Easy Scallop™
▶ Freezer paper

Block Assembly

Make 48(100) blocks

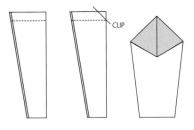

Step 1. Cut all the wedges with the Easy Dresden tool (or use the template on page 118). Fold the widest edge of the wedge right sides together. Stitch across the top with a ¼" seam. Trim off the corner at the fold to reduce bulk. Turn, center seam, and press.

> **Tip:** The bamboo point turner is ideal for turning the points.

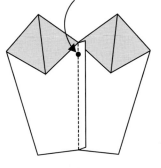

Start stitching here, backstitch to edge, then stitch seam.

Step 2. Sew a variety of five wedges together for each fan. Make 96(200) fans. When joining two wedges, begin stitching ½" below the two folded edges of the wedges. Backstitch to the folds, then finish sewing the seam. This effectively hides the thread ends behind the piecing. Press the seams in each fan all in one direction.

Step 3. Machine or hand baste a fan in one corner of the 8½" yellow background block. The base of the fan should be an equal distance from the corner of the block on both edges. Run a line of basting across the top edge of the fan, down one side and across the base of the fan.

> **Note:** The top edge of the fan is only basted down and does not need to be appliquéd down. The quilting that is done later will hold the fan into place.

Make 48 (100)

Cutting Directions

From	Cut	To Yield
Yellow solid	12(25)—8½" strips	48(100)—8½" squares
	8(10)—6" strips	Outside borders
Variety of prints	40(84)—4" x 21" strips	480(1000) wedges cut with Easy Dresden*
Dark blue solid	6(12)—2½" strips	96(200)—2½" squares, then using the template in the Easy Dresden package (or page 118), round off one corner for the fan base
	7(10)—1½" strips	Inside border
	1¼" bias strips	Binding to make 320"

*****Note:** If not using Easy Dresden, use the templates on page 118.

Step 4. Baste a second fan in the opposite corner of the block.

Step 5. A template for the fan base is given in the directions with the Easy Dresden tool (and on page 118). Trace onto firm cardboard or template plastic. To speed up the process of cutting and appliquéing the fan bases, cut several 2¼" strips of freezer paper. Cut into squares, then using the template, round off one corner to make the fan base. You can cut several of these freezer paper templates at once, and they can be used several times before discarding.

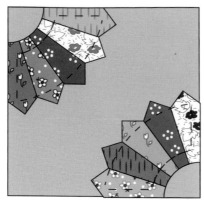

Make 48 (100)

Step 6. Place the freezer paper fan bases on the blue squares, matching the corner and edges. Iron to the wrong side of the blue fabric. With a scissors, cut the curved edge adding a scant ¼" seam allowance to the curved edge. Now you can finger or iron press the blue fabric over the curved edge of the freezer paper.

Tip: *A little spray starch can help to give a crisp turned-under edge. Once that edge is sufficiently pressed, the freezer paper template can be removed. Appliqué the fan base to the fans by hand or machine.*

Step 7. Sew the blocks together in eight(10) rows of six(10) blocks each. Press the seams in alternating directions by rows.

Note: *There is always a fan in the upper left-hand corner of the block.*

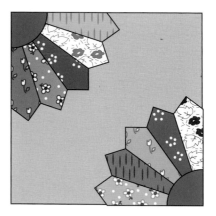

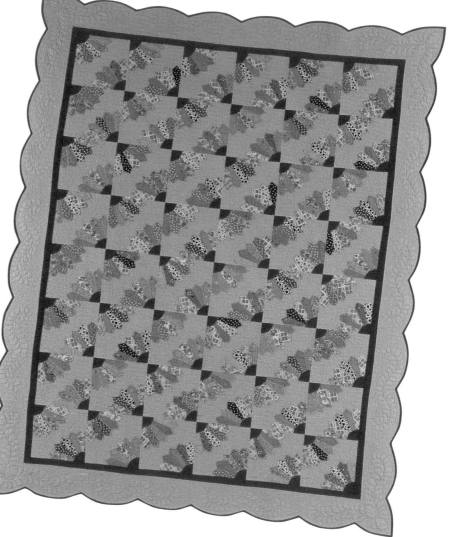

Borders

Step 1. Measure the width of the quilt. Piece two narrow blue borders to this measurement. Sew to the top and bottom of the quilt center and press toward the blue border. (See page 14 for more instruction on adding borders.)

Step 2. Measure the length of the quilt. Piece two narrow blue borders to this measurement. Sew to the sides of the quilt center and press toward the blue border.

Step 3. Measure, cut, and sew the wider yellow borders in the same manner.

Finishing Directions

Cut batting and backing several inches larger than the top. Mark any quilting designs, then layer, baste, and quilt. The quilt shown was machine-quilted in a meander in all the yellow open areas. The fans were stitched ¼" from the seam allowances. A feather design was stitched in the border, and the background filled in with meandering.

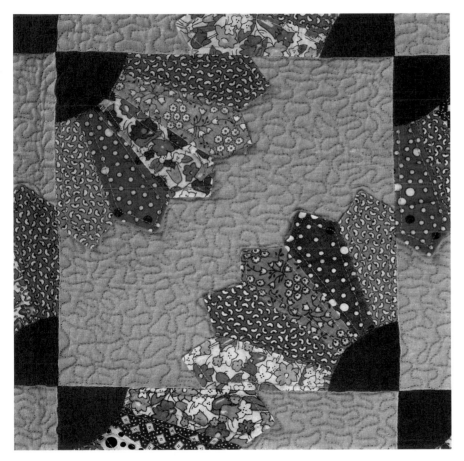

Scalloped Edge Finish

Mark the scalloped edge on the quilt. The quilt shown was marked with 7½" scallops. (See page 126 for marking and binding the scalloped edge.) Bind with dark blue single bias binding cut at 1¼".

Don't forget to sign and date your quilt!

Leaf Tablecloth

(70" round)

Machine appliquéd by author.

For a quick decorating project, purchase a plain, white cotton tablecloth to fit your table. Follow the directions given to appliqué this tablecloth and add the perfect touch to your next garden party!

Appliqué the Tablecloth

Step 1. Iron the tablecloth to remove the creases. Fold the tablecloth in half, press lightly in the center, and fold again and press to mark the quarters. Create a master template (see page 119) for positioning the stems of the leaf block.

Step 2. Following the directions on page 55 - 56 for the Feedsack Leaf quilt and using the pressed lines at the quarters and your master template, position and fuse or stitch the leaves in place. Prepare two stems. Position, baste, and then stitch in place.

Step 3. To mark a scallop border on any size tablecloth, measure the circumference of the tablecloth 3" inside the hem to allow for the scallop. (See the sidebar for more information on determining circumference.) Choose the number of scallops (I chose 18), divide circumference by 18 (201" divided by 18 = 11.16"). Round to 11¼" and set your scallop tool or mark intervals approximately that far apart along the border. Adjust the last few scallops as needed.

Note: *I do not mark into the finished hem of the tablecloth. That is cut away after the binding is sewn on the scalloped edge. If you wish to keep as much of the length as possible, open up the hem before marking the scallop, and take that extra length into consideration when figuring the circumference of the tablecloth.*

Step 4. Using the tips of one branch of the master template, position and mark a cluster of three leaves about ½" above the "V" in each of the scallops (leaving room for the binding). Fuse or appliqué the leaves into position.

Binding

Cut 1¼" green solid bias strips. Join with diagonal seams pressed open. You will need approximately a 220" length for binding the 70" round tablecloth. Bind, following the directions on page 126.

Washing Instructions

To completely remove the blue marks, any glue or starch, soak the tablecloth in cold water. Rinse, then spin. (Do not agitate). Allow to dry flat. Iron as needed.

Dainty Cakestands Quilt

Size shown: (63" x 74"), 8" finished block; queen-size: (101" x 101")
Reproduction fabrics, pieced and machine-quilted by author.

This lovely quilt features a favorite basket block called Cakestands. In the days before electric mixers and store-bought cake mixes, a measure of a housewife's cooking ability was shown in how well she could bake a cake. Cakes graced the table at many family events and whenever company was present. These cakes were often prominently displayed on lovely footed glass cake stands.

This dainty feminine quilt is reminiscent of those bygone days and fancy cakes on glass cake stands.

Directions for a queen-size quilt are included (in parentheses).

Fabric Requirements

▶ Vintage white: 1⅛ yd. (2⅓ yd.)
▶ Yellow solid: 2 yd. (3½ yd.)
▶ Blue solid: 1¼ yd. (1⅓ yd.)
▶ Yellow/blue print for border: 2⅓ yd. (3¼ yd.)
▶ Variety of prints: 16 fat quarters (2 baskets each) OR for queen-size: 22 fat quarters (4 baskets each)

Suggested Tools

▶ Easy Angle™
▶ Companion Angle™
▶ Easy Scallop™

Block Assembly

Make 32(85) blocks: 12(36) with white background, 20(49) with yellow background.

Step 1. Assemble the four small triangle-squares. Press toward the print triangle. Assemble one large triangle-square.

Make 4   Make 1

Step 2. Join the small triangle squares from Step 1 into pairs, facing in opposite directions as shown. Add a solid square to the right of the first pair as shown.

Step 3. Sew the second pair to the side of the larger triangle square.

Step 4. Sew the first pair to the top of the previous unit.

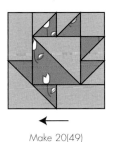

Step 5. Sew a print triangle to two background rectangles, facing in opposite directions as shown.

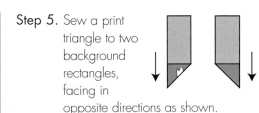

Step 6. Sew the rectangle units to the sides of the basket.

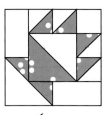

Step 7. Sew a large background triangle to the base of the basket. Repeat to make 12(36) baskets with white background, and 20(49) baskets with yellow background.

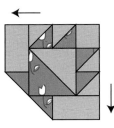

Make 20(49)   Make 12(36)

Cutting Directions for Basket Blocks

From	Cut	To Yield
Vintage white	2(5)—4½" strips	24(72) Easy Angle** triangles
	3(8)— 2½" strips	48(144) Easy Angle** triangles*
		12(36)—2½" squares
Yellow solid	2(5)— 4½" strips	24(72)—2½" x 4½" rectangles
	3(7)— 4½" strips	40(98) Easy Angle** triangles
	5(11)—2½" strips	80(196) Easy Angle** triangles*
		20(49) 2½" squares
	3(7)— 4½" strips	40(98) 2½" x 4½" rectangles
From each print	1— 4½" x 6"(12")	2(4) Easy Angle** triangles
	1(2)—2½" x 21"	12(24) Easy Angle** triangles*

*Layer 2½" white(yellow) and print strips right sides together and cut eight(16) small triangle sets for each print. Cut an additional four(eight) more print triangles for the base of the baskets without the white(yellow) strip.

Note: If not using Easy Angle, cut 4⅞" and 2⅞" squares respectively, cut once on the diagonal.

Assembling the Quilt

Step 1. Sew a yellow triangle to one side of a white square, sewing with the square on top to prevent stretching the bias edge of the triangle.

Step 2. Press toward the yellow triangle. Add a second yellow triangle to an adjacent edge of the white square to form a large triangle.

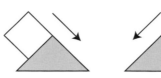

Make 14(24) large triangles

 Note: *The pieced triangle will be larger than needed.*

Step 3. Lay out the blocks in diagonal rows, using the pieced setting triangles along the edges. Sew the blocks and triangles together in diagonal rows. Press the seams in each row in alternating directions.

Step 4. Sew the rows together. Press the seams all one direction. Add the yellow corner triangles last.

 Note: *The corner triangles are larger than needed, center them on the quilt corners.*

Step 5. Trim the edges of the quilt straight, leaving ¼" from the corner of the blocks, and keeping the corners square.

Borders

Step 1. Piece the narrow blue solid border as needed with diagonal seams pressed open. Trim two borders the width of the quilt. Sew the borders to the top and bottom of the quilt. Press the seams toward the borders. (See page 14 for more instruction on adding borders.)

Step 2. Repeat for the sides of the quilt.

Step 3. Trim two yellow/blue print borders to the width of the quilt. Sew to the top and bottom of the quilt. Press toward the wide borders. Trim two yellow/blue borders to the length of the quilt plus borders. Sew to the sides of the quilt. Press toward the wide borders.

Finishing the Quilt

Step 1. Using Easy Scallop (directions on page 126), mark the scallop edge on the quilt. I marked a 9" scallop on the top and bottom of the quilt, and a 9¼" scallop on the sides. (Adjust the sizes as needed for the larger quilt.)

Step 2. Layer, baste, and quilt. The quilt shown was machine meandered in all the white and yellow background areas. Hand-quilting ¼" from the seam lines was stitched in the large print triangle in each basket. The narrow border was stitched in the ditch on both sides. The wide border had a large meander quilted in it.

Binding

Join the 1¼" bias strips with diagonal seams pressed open. Before binding, hand or machine baste (with a walking foot!) along the marked edge. This will prevent the layers from stretching or shifting while the binding is being sewn on. Sew the binding to the scalloped edge. (See page 126 for instructions on binding a scalloped edge.) Trim, then turn the binding to the back side and stitch down by hand with matching thread.

Sign and date your Cakestands quilt.

Cutting Directions for Setting Triangles, Border, and Binding

From	Cut	To Yield
Vintage white	2(3)—4½" strips	14(24)—4½" squares
Yellow solid	4(6)—3½" strips	28(48) Companion Angle* triangles
	2—7" squares	Cut once on the diagonal to make 4 corner triangles
Blue solid	6(8)—1½" strips	Inside border
	1¼" bias strips	Single bias binding to make 320"(425")
Yellow/blue print	4—8½" x 78" (10½" x 108")	Outside borders cut lengthwise

*Note: If not using Companion Angle, cut 7(12)—7¼" squares, cut twice on the diagonal to make 28(48) triangles.

Dainty Cakestands Pillow

12" square without ruffle

Pieced and machine-quilted by author.

With a leftover block from the Dainty Cakestands Quilt (or make up a new block!), you can create this lovely pillow for instant decorating in any room of the house.

Fabric Requirements

▸ Dark green print: 1¼ yd.
▸ Medium green print: fat eighth
▸ Vintage white: fat eighth
▸ 14" square of batting and muslin
▸ 12" pillow form

Suggested Tool

▸ Easy Angle™

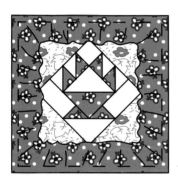

Block Assembly

Step 1. Follow the directions for piecing the Cakestands block on page 25. Center, pin, and sew the medium green print triangles to all sides of the basket block. At this point, the block should measure 12½".

Step 2. Layer the block, batting, and muslin. Baste, then quilt as desired. The pillow shown was machine meandered in the white background and stitched in the ditch around the green triangles. Echo quilting in a chevron pattern completed the cakestand, and three parallel lines finished the corner pieces. Baste a scant ¼" from the edge to keep the layers from shifting.

Pillow Back

Fold the 12½" x 16" rectangles in half, wrong sides together, to form two 12½" x 8" pillow backs. Overlap to form a 12½" square. Baste a scant ¼" around the edges of the pillow back to hold it together.

Pillow Ruffle

Trim off selvages and join the short ends of the ruffle strips to make a continuous strip. Press the seams open, then fold the ruffle strip in half, wrong sides together and press. Divide into four equal sections and mark with a safety pin. Gather the ruffle with double basting thread or sew over quilting thread with a zig-zag stitch. Gather the ruffle to fit the pillow, allowing extra fullness at the corners and matching the safety pins on the ruffle with each corner of the pillow. Baste the ruffle to the pillow with a ¼" seam.

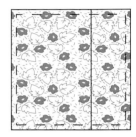

 Tip: *Round the corners when sewing on the ruffle and when sewing the top and back together. The rounded corners are easier to sew and will look better when the pillow is finished.*

Finishing the Pillow

With the ruffle sandwiched in between the pillow top and pillow back, pin and sew the layers together with a ⅜" seam. Trim the corners, then turn the pillow right side out through the opening in the pillow back. Tuck in a 12" pillow form and you are finished!

Cutting Directions

From	Cut	To Yield
Vintage white	1—4½" x 20"	2—4½" Easy Angle* triangles
		2—2½" x 4½" rectangles
	1—2½" x 20"	4—2½" Easy Angle* triangles
		1—2½" square
Medium green	1—6½" x 20"	4—6½" Easy Angle* triangles
Dark green	1—4½" x 42"	1—4½" Easy Angle* triangle. Trim remainder of strip to 2½", cut 6—2½" Easy Angle* triangles
	1—12½" x 42"	2—12½" x 16" rectangles for pillow back
	3—7" x 42"	Double ruffle strips

***Note:** If not using Easy Angle, cut 4⅞" and 2⅞" squares respectively.*

Flower Garden Table Runner

(18" x 36½")

Machine-pieced and hand- and machine-quilted by author.

Using just three blocks from the Almost a Flower Garden Quilt pattern (page 68), you can quickly make up these lovely garden-themed table runners to brighten up your table or to give as gifts.

For an alternate look, try substituting red (or another favorite color) for the blue in the table runner.

Block Assembly

Make 3 blocks

Step 1. Make three blocks according to the directions on page 69. Trim to 9" square. Join the blocks in a row with solid blue sashing between the blocks.

Step 2. Sew narrow solid blue borders to the quilt. Press toward the narrow border. (See page 14 for more instruction on adding borders.)

Step 3. Sew 4" wide print borders to the table runner. Press toward the last border added.

Finishing the Quilt

Step 1. Mark any quilting designs on the quilt top. Mark the scallop border with the blue washout pen or chalk. The table runners shown were scalloped with a 6" scallop. The red table runner was marked with half scallops at the corners, while the blue table runner was marked with full scallops at each corner. (See instructions on page 126 for marking scalloped borders.)

Step 2. Layer, baste, and quilt. The quilt shown was hand-quilted ¼" from the seam lines following the rings in the "flowers," and was machine stitched in the ditch on both sides of the narrow sashes and border. A large meander was quilted in the print border.

Binding

Step 1. Before binding, hand baste a scant ¼" from the edge of the quilt, or along the marked scalloped line if making scalloped edges. This will prevent the layers from shifting or stretching while the binding is being attached.

Step 2. Prepare a bias 1¼" blue binding by joining the short ends with a diagonal seam pressed open. Sew the binding to the quilt. (See page 126 for more instruction on binding a scalloped edge.)

Step 3. Turn the binding to the back side of the quilt and stitch down by hand.

Cutting Directions

From	Cut	To Yield
Yellow solid	2" x 8" strip	3 — 2" squares for flower centers
Pink solid	2" x 26" strip	12 — 2" squares for flowers
Each blue print	2" strip	2 — 2" x 5" rectangles
		6 — 2" x 3½" rectangles
		2 — 2" squares
Vintage white	2 — 1¾" strips	36 Companion Angle* triangles
	1 — 2" strip	12 Easy Angle** triangles for block corners
Light blue solid	3 — 1½" strips	Sashing and inner border
	1¼" bias strips	Binding to make 150"
Blue print	3 — 4" strips	Outer border

*Note: If not using Companion Angle, cut nine 3¾" squares. Cut twice on the diagonal.

**If not using Easy Angle, cut six 2⅜" squares. Cut once on the diagonal.

Friendship Baskets Wall Quilt

Size shown: (34" x 41"), 5" finished block; lap quilt: (51" x 62"), 7½" finished block
Reproduction fabrics pieced and hand- and machine-quilted by author.

Friendship quilts have a long and interesting history. For at least 150 years signature quilts have been given to commemorate a special event in a person's life (retirement, anniversary, wedding, birthday, etc.), as a farewell gift for someone moving away or retiring from a job, or just out of friendship. The gorgeous and innovative appliquéd Baltimore Album quilts made in the mid-1800s were usually signature quilts, but there are humbler examples as well. Often quilts with signatures or Bible verses were given when a family headed west and were no doubt a consolation for that family when they were far away from loved ones.

Signature quilts were also made for young men when they turned 21. Often these were called "Freedom Quilts," because when a young man came of age—turned 21—his labor and earnings no longer belonged to his father. Women of the same era didn't receive the same freedom. Their belongings and labor were the property of their father before marriage, and their husband after marriage.

Need a special quilt for someone in your life that is celebrating a special birthday, anniversary, wedding, or another important event? This quick-to-make quilt will be a treasured gift with the addition of signatures of friends and relatives. The inside triangle border is a breeze to make, and the triangles are echoed in the prairie point edging. If you'd like to make a larger size, see the directions page 36 for a quilt with a 7½" finished block. This quilt will also make up quickly for that special event!

Fabric Requirements

▶ Vintage white: 1½ yd.
▶ Variety of prints: 16 fat quarters

Suggested Tools and Supplies

▶ Easy Angle™
▶ Companion Angle™
▶ Pigma permanent pen for signatures

Block Assembly

Make 32 blocks

 Tip: *Put all the pieces you need for one block on a paper plate. Do this for all the blocks, stacking the paper plates. Then, when you have a few minutes to sew, you can piece a block or two quickly.*

Step 1. Using the white 2½" Easy Angle triangle, sew the 1" x 3½" print rectangle to the bottom of the triangle.

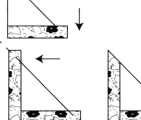

Note: *The rectangle is longer than needed.*

Step 2. Sew the 1" x 4" print rectangle to the remaining short side of the triangle. Trim the entire triangle to the 3½" size on the Easy Angle tool.

Step 3. Sew the pieced triangle to the large print triangle.

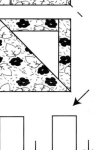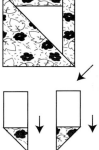

Step 4. Sew the small print triangles to the ends of the white 1½" x 2½" rectangles, having the triangles positioned as shown.

Cutting Directions

From	Cut	To Yield
Vintage white	3—2½" strips	64 Easy Angle* triangles
	4—1½" strips	64—1½" x 2½" rectangles
	4—1½" strips	32—1½" x 4½" rectangles
	5—1½" strips	32—1½" x 5½" rectangles
	2—3" strips	14—3" squares for setting triangles
	2—1¾" strips	36—1¾" squares for setting triangles
	4—3½" strips	Outer border
From each print (enough for 2 blocks)	1—3½" x 21" strip	2 Easy Angle* triangles; trim remainder of strip to 3"; cut 5—3" squares for prairie points
	1—1½" x 21" strip	4 Easy Angle* triangles for baskets 5 Companion Angle** triangles for borders
	1—1" x 21" strip	2—1" x 3½" rectangles for handles 2—1" x 4" rectangles for handles

***Note:** *If not using Easy Angle, cut 2⅞", 1⅞", and 3⅞" squares respectively, cut once on the diagonal.*

***If not using Companion Angle, cut 3¼" squares, cut twice on the diagonal.*

Step 5. Sew those units to adjacent sides of the basket.

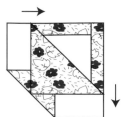

Step 6. Sew the white 2½" Easy Angle triangle to the base of the basket, and the white rectangles to adjacent sides at the top of the basket. At this point, the basket block should measure 5½". Repeat to make a total of 32 baskets.

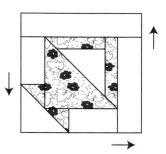

Pieced Inner Border

Step 1. Sew small print Companion Angle triangles to adjacent sides of the 1¾" white squares.

Make 36 pieced triangle units.

Step 2. In the same manner, sew two of the pieced triangle units to adjacent sides of the white 3" squares.

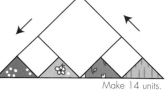

Make 14 units.

Step 3. Sew the remaining pieced triangle units together to make 4 corner units as shown.

Step 4. Arrange the basket blocks and the large pieced triangles in diagonal rows. Note that the setting triangles are larger than needed and can be trimmed later. Join the units in each row, pressing the seams in each row all one direction, but alternating the direction from row to row. Sew the rows together to make the quilt top. Add the corner units last.

Borders

Step 1. Trim the sides of the quilt if needed to straighten the edges. Be certain to leave at least ¼" from the corners for seam allowance and keep the corners at 90 degree angles.

Step 2. Measure and trim two white borders the width of the quilt. Sew to the top and bottom of the quilt. Press toward the borders. (See page 14 for more instruction on adding borders.)

Step 3. Repeat for the side borders.

Prairie Point Edging

Step 1. Cut four more 3" squares from your prints.

Step 2. Fold each of the 3" print squares in half on the diagonal. Press. Fold the resulting triangle in half, pressing again.

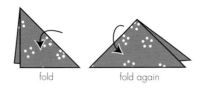
fold   fold again

Step 3. Positioning one inside of another, baste together 19 prairie points for the top and bottom borders, adjusting to fit. The prairie points at either end should come right to the corners of the white borders.

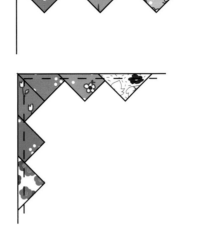

Step 4. With the prairie points pointing to the inside of the quilt, sew to the edge of the quilt with a ¼" seam. Repeat with 23 prairie points for the sides. When opened, the prairie points at the corners should make a straight line.

Finishing the Quilt

Step 1. Mark any quilting lines, then baste the three layers together. Quilt as desired. The quilt shown was machine meandered in the background and hand-quilted in a chain pattern in the border.

Step 2. Trim the batting ¼" shorter than the quilt top. Trim the backing even with the raw edge of the quilt top (with the prairie points pointing in). Open out the prairie points and fold the backing over ¼" so it covers the stitching line on the back side of the prairie points. Stitch the backing in place by hand.
Your quilt is now finished, enjoy!

Fabric Requirements

▶ Vintage white: 3 yd.
▶ Prints: 16 fat quarters

Suggested Tools and Supplies

▶ Easy Angle™
▶ Companion Angle™
▶ Pigma permanent pen for signatures

Lap Quilt:

(51" x 62")

▶ 7½" finished block, 4 x 5 setting, 32 blocks

▶ Follow directions as for the smaller quilt.

Have friends or relatives add their signatures to this quilt to create a treasured keepsake.

Cutting Directions

From	Cut	To Yield
Vintage white	4—3½" strips	64 Easy Angle* triangles*
	6—2" strips	64—2" x 3½" rectangles
	6—2" strips	32—2" x 6½" rectangles
	7—2" strips	32—2" x 8" rectangles
	2—4½" strips	14—4½" squares for setting triangles
	3—2½" strips	36—2½" squares for setting triangles
	7—4½" strips	Outer border

From each print you will be cutting enough pieces for two blocks as well as the border triangles and prairie points.

From each print	1—5" x 21" strip	2 Easy Angle* triangles; trim remainder of strip to 4"; cut 4—4" squares for prairie points***
	1—2" x 21" strip	4 Easy Angle* triangles
		5 Companion Angle** triangles for borders
	1—1¼" x 21" strip	2—1¼" x 4½" rectangles
		2—1¼" x 5½" rectangles

***Note:** If not using Easy Angle, cut 3⅞" squares, 5⅜" squares, and 2⅜" squares respectively and cut once on the diagonal.*

***If not using Companion Angle, cut 4¼" squares, cut twice on the diagonal.*

****You will need to cut a few more squares from the prints for the prairie points.*

The Kitchen

Picnic Basket Cherries Wall Quilt

42" square, 9" finished block
Reproduction fabrics hand-appliquéd, machine-pieced, and hand-quilted by author.

Don't you just love the freshness of these cherries set with the tiny red check? Makes one think of long, lazy days of summer and picnics…

The inspiration for this quilt came from a vintage Aunt Martha's pattern for fruit tea towels. I adapted the cherry design for this quilt, a table runner, potholders, and kitchen curtains. Fruit designs were popular some 50 or more years ago, and today are delighting women once again.

Fabric Requirements

▶ Vintage white: ⅞ yd.
▶ Red check: 1⅝ yd.
▶ Red solid: 1 yd. (includes binding)
▶ Green solid: 2" x 24" strip

Suggested Tools and Supplies

▶ Easy Angle™
▶ Shape Cut™
▶ Easy Scallop™
▶ Freezer paper or fusible web
▶ Green embroidery floss
▶ Blue washout pen

Cherry Blocks

Make 5

Step 1. Using the pattern on page 118, make a 9" template for the red check border. To do this, cut a 9" square of freezer paper or fusible web. Transfer the border pattern to the paper side of the freezer paper. Cut out on the marked line. Iron to the wrong side of the red check squares. Cut out, adding a scant ¼" seam allowance on the inside shaped edge. If using freezer paper, clip all inside curves, then with the point of the iron, turn the edges over the freezer paper. (See pages 12 to 13 for more instruction on traditional appliqué and fusible web appliqué.)

Step 2. Glue baste, pin, or thread baste (or fuse if using fusible web) the red check border over the smaller white square. Appliqué in place by hand or machine with matching (or invisible) thread. Repeat to make a total of five blocks.

Step 3. Trace the cherry and leaf design (page 118) on the paper side of fusible web or the dull side of freezer paper. Appliqué or fuse the cherries and leaves in place. With an outline stitch and two strands of green floss, embroider the cherry stems. See page 13 for outline stitch.

 Tip: *I use a blue washout pen to mark the appliqué placement on the background so any marks that aren't covered with fabric will be washed away later. Just DO NOT iron over the blue marks, as it will set them permanently!*

Step 4. When all the blocks are finished, soak in cold water to remove any starch and blue washout pen marks. Dry flat, then press the blocks right side down on a terry cloth towel.

Cutting Directions for Cherry Blocks

From	Cut	To Yield
Vintage white	1—6½" strip	5—6½" squares
Red check	2—9" strips	5—9" squares

Basket Blocks

Make 4

Step 1. Sew the red solid squares, the red check square, and small check triangles together in three rows as shown. Sew the rows together to make the basket base.

Make 4

Step 2. Sew the red solid triangles to the ends of the white rectangles as shown, making four of each.

Make 4 →   ← Make 4

Step 3. Sew these to the sides of the basket base, pressing as shown.

Step 4. Sew the smaller white triangle to the bottom of the basket.

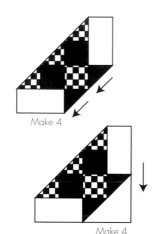

Make 4

Make 4

Step 5. Trace the basket handle pattern (page 123) four times on either fusible web or freezer paper. Follow the detailed directions on pages 12 to 13 for fusing or appliquéing the handle to the large white triangles. When the appliqué is complete, sew the handle section of the basket to the base of the basket. Press.

Make 4

Step 6. Center, pin, and then sew the large red check triangles to opposite sides of the basket block. (They will be slightly larger than needed.) Press toward the red triangles. Repeat on the remaining two sides. Press toward the triangles. Trim the entire block evenly to 9", including seam allowances.

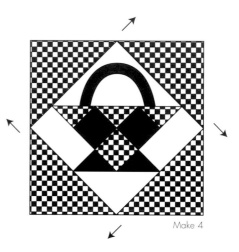

Make 4

Cutting Directions for Basket Blocks

From	Cut	To Yield
Vintage white	1— 5" strip	4 Easy Angle* triangles. Trim strip to 3½", cut 4 more Easy Angle* triangles
	1—2" strip	8—2" x 3½" rectangles
Red check	2—5" strips	16 Easy Angle* triangles
	1—2" strip	12 Easy Angle* triangles
		4—2" squares
Red solid	1—2" strip	8 Easy Angle* triangles
		8—2" squares
	1—3" strip	4 basket handles

*__Note:__ *If not using Easy Angle, cut your strips ⅜" wider. Cut squares, then cut once on the diagonal to make the triangles.*

Sashing Assembly

Step 1. Sew together six strip sets of white/red solid/white. Press toward the red. Cut into 24—9" sashings. Cut 16—1" wide units from the remainder of these strips for the nine-patch corner squares.

Step 2. Sew together one strip set of red solid/white/red solid. Press toward the red. Cut into 32—1" wide units for the nine-patch corner squares. Assemble 16 nine-patch corner squares with these units and those from Step 1.

Step 3. Referring to the photo on page 38, sew the blocks together with the sashing in three horizontal rows. Press toward the sashing.

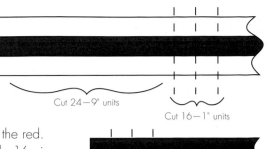

Cut 24—9" units

Cut 16—1" units

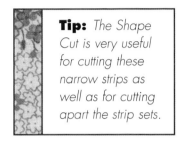

Cut 32—1" units

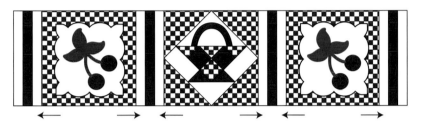

Tip: The Shape Cut is very useful for cutting these narrow strips as well as for cutting apart the strip sets.

Step 4. Sew the sashing and corner squares together in four horizontal rows. Press toward the sashing.

Step 5. Join the block rows and sashing rows. Press toward the sashing.

Borders

Step 1. Mitered corners look nice on this quilt. To make mitered corners, follow the directions on page 14, using the red check 5½" strips.

Step 2. Mark a scalloped edge on the quilt. The quilt shown was marked in 6" scallops. See page 126 for instruction on marking a scalloped edge.

Sashing and Border Cutting Directions

From	Cut	To Yield
Vintage white	13—1" strips	Strip sets
Red solid	8—1" strips	Strip sets
	1¼" bias strips	210" bias binding
Red check	4—5½" strips	Borders

Finishing the Quilt

Step 1. Layer, baste, and quilt as desired. The quilt shown was quilted along the seam lines and echoing the shapes of the designs. Cross-hatching was done in the border.

Step 2. Bind the scalloped edge with red solid bias binding cut at 1¼". See page 126 for instruction on binding a scalloped edge.
Sign and date your picnic quilt!

Sweet Cherries Table Runner

(17" x 37"), 6" finished block

Machine-pieced and quilted with reproduction fabrics by author.

Taking the cherry motif from the Picnic Basket Cherries Wall Quilt, I created this cheery table runner. Just simple checkerboard squares alternated with the cherry blocks makes for an interesting (and quick and easy) table runner!

Cherry Blocks

Make 3

Step 1. Trace the cherries and leaves (page 118) onto freezer paper or fusible web. Appliqué or fuse the shapes in place on the 6½" white squares. (If fusing, stitch around the shapes so the table runner can be laundered.) See pages 12 to 13 for more instructions on appliqué and fusing.

Step 2. Trace the stems onto the squares; embroider with two strands of green floss.

Checkerboard Blocks

Step 1. Using the 2½" strips, sew together a strip set of red check/white/red check. Press toward the red check. Cut into 14—2½" segments.

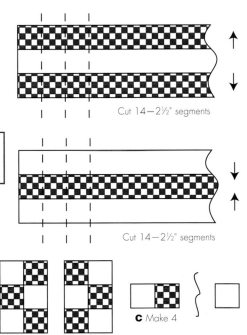

Cut 14—2½" segments

Cut 14—2½" segments

> **Tip:** The Shape Cut will work great for cutting apart those segments!

Step 2. Sew together a strip set of white/red check/white. Press toward the red check strip. Cut into 14—2½" segments.

Step 3. Using the segments from Step 1 and 2, sew together four nine-patches (A). Also join two segments to form six partial blocks (B). Remove one square from the remaining strip set segments (C).

A Make 4   B Make 6   C Make 4

Step 4. Cut the four white 4¼" squares twice on the diagonal to make 16 triangles. You will only need 14 triangles.

Step 5. Using the red check squares and the white triangles, construct four D units like this, pressing toward the red square.

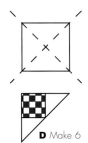

D Make 6

Cutting Directions

From	Cut	To Yield
Vintage white	1—6½" strip	3—6½" squares
		4—4¼" squares
	3—2½" strips	Checkerboard
Red check	4—2½" strips	Checkerboard
		6—2½" squares
Red solid	3—2¼" strips	Binding

Step 6. Using a unit D from Step 5, and a unit C from Step 3, construct four units like this:

Make 4

Step 7. Using two units from Step 6, add white triangles to make two units like this:

Make 2

Step 8. Using two partial block B's from Step 3, and a D unit from Step 5, assemble two rows like this:

Make 2

Step 9. Using a partial block B from Step 3, a cherry block, a block A, and a unit from Step 7, assemble two rows like this:

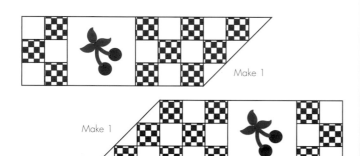

Make 1

Make 1

Step 10. Using two block A's, a cherry block, and two units from Step 6, assemble the center row like this:

Make 1

Step 11. Lay out the rows in order, then sew together, matching and pinning the seam intersections.

Finishing the Quilt

Step 1. Cut the batting and backing several inches larger than the table runner. Baste together, then quilt as desired. The table runner shown was hand-quilted around the appliqué motifs and diagonal lines were quilted through the red squares. The white areas were machine stippled.

Step 2. Before binding, hand or machine baste a scant ¼" from the edge of the table runner. This will keep the edges from distorting or shifting while the binding is being attached.

Step 3. Join the binding strips with diagonal seams pressed open. Fold the binding wrong sides together along the length and press. Sew the binding to the table runner with a ¼" seam. Trim off the excess batting and backing and stitch the binding to the back side by hand with matching thread. (See page 15 for more instructions on binding.) Sign and date your Sweet Cherries table runner!

This vintage Aunt Martha's transfer was the inspiration for all of the cherry projects.

Cherry Curtains

(12½" x 84")

Pieced and machine appliquéd by author.

Wouldn't these curtains add a bright touch to your kitchen? Making your own curtains would follow a long tradition of women who made curtains and decorated their own homes. These curtains are especially easy to do as the lining is incorporated with the curtains. If you would like to change the width of the curtains to fit your windows, cut the curtain fabric twice the width of your window.

Fabric Requirements

- ▶ Vintage white: 1⅛ yd.
- ▶ Red check: ½ yd.
- ▶ Red solid: scraps or fat eighth
- ▶ Green solid: scraps or fat eighth

Additional Supplies

- ▶ Fusible web
- ▶ Black thread or embroidery floss for buttonhole stitch
- ▶ Green embroidery floss for stems
- ▶ One package red rick-rack: jumbo, ⅝" wide

Assembly Directions

Step 1. Using the pattern for the cherry/leaf branch on page 118, trace 16 cherries on the paper side of the fusible web, and 16 of one leaf and eight of another. Fuse the cherry circles to the back side of the red fabric and the leaves to the back side of the green solid fabric. Cut out on the marked line. (See page 13 for more directions on fusible appliqué.)

Step 2. Reverse and trace the cherry design onto a sheet of paper. Use this under the curtain fabric for a placement guide. The first cherry motif should be placed 7" from the edge of the curtain to the center of the motif, and about 1" up from the seam. Fuse in place. Continue positioning and fusing the cherry motifs about 10" apart from the center of each motif, ending with the last one about 7" from the end.

Step 3. With a quilt marking pencil, lightly mark the stem lines. Embroider with two strands of green floss.

Step 4. With black thread or floss, buttonhole stitch around the cherries and leaves.

Step 5. Sew the red rick-rack over the seam between the red check and the white fabrics. Press the short ends of the curtain under ⅜".

Step 6. With right sides together, sew the red check section to the other end of the white section, making a tube! Press the seam to the red check. Turn the tube right sides out, folding the red check in half and matching the seams; press.

Step 7. To make the pocket for the curtain rod, mark your sewing machine 1¼" to the right of the needle. This will be your first sewing guide. Stitch along the top white edge 1¼" from the fold. Backstitch at each end.

Step 8. Mark another line 2½" to the right of the needle. Use this as your second sewing guide. Backstitch at each end. (This will form the pocket for the curtain rod.)

Step 9. Matching up the folded edges on the short sides, begin top-stitching the curtain ends together at the second line of sewing and stitch to the fold at the bottom of the curtain. (DO NOT sew across the curtain rod pocket!) Backstitch. Do this on both ends.

Step 10. Insert curtain rod, hang and enjoy!

Cutting Directions

- ▶ Cut two 19" x 42" strips of white. Sew end-to-end with the seam pressed open.

- ▶ Cut two 7" x 42" strips of red check. Sew end to end with the seam pressed open. Sew the long edge of the red check strip to one long edge of the white strip. Press the seam toward the red strip.

Cherry Potholders

9" square. (Makes 2)
Machine pieced by author.

For a cheerful bit of color in your kitchen, make up these
sweet cherry potholders—they are as easy as pie!

Fabric Requirements

▶ Vintage white: 7" x 14"
▶ Red check: ½ yd.
▶ Red solid: ¼ yd.
▶ Green solid: scraps

Additional Requirements

▶ Fusible webbing
▶ 1 package red rick-rack: ½" wide
▶ Green and black embroidery floss
▶ 4—10" squares of cotton batting

Block Assembly

Step 1. Trace four cherries and six leaves from the pattern on page 118 on the paper side of fusible webbing. Roughly cut out the shapes. Iron to the wrong side of the green and red solid fabrics. Cut out and fuse to the white squares to make two block centers. (See page 13 for directions on fusible appliqué.) Add the embroidered stems and machine or hand-buttonhole stitch around each of the shapes with black thread or floss.

Step 2. Sew the 2" x 6" red check rectangles on opposite sides of the appliquéd squares. Press toward the check borders. Add the 2" x 9½" red check rectangles to the remaining sides and press.

Step 3. With matching thread, sew the rick-rack over the seam lines, extending to the edges of the potholder.

Finishing the Potholders

Step 1. Layer the backing, two layers of cotton batting, and the blocks. Quilt the center of the potholders if desired. The examples were machine meandered in the white area.

Step 2. Baste a scant ¼" around the edges to keep the layers together. Prepare double, straight-of-grain binding. Sew to the potholders with a ¼" seam. Trim excess batting and backing; turn the binding to the back side and stitch down by hand with matching thread.

Step 3. A loop of rick-rack can be tacked to the back for a hanger if desired.

Cutting Directions

From	Cut	To Yield
Vintage white	2—6" squares	Potholder centers
Red check	1—10" strip	2—10" squares for potholder backs
	2—2" strips	4—2" x 6" rectangles
		4—2" x 9½" rectangles
Red solid	2—2¼" strips	Binding

Feedsack Patches Quilt

(38" x 48")

Quilt shown was pieced by the author and hand-quilted by Pam Kienholz.

I have been buying, selling, and collecting feedsacks for years. Several years ago I decided to reduce my stash of feedsacks, so I designed a quilt that would showcase a wide variety of prints. I had so much fun making the quilt, I thought others would too! The pattern was sent to American Patchwork and Quilting magazine—and I offered a kit to make the little quilt. I never dreamed it would be so popular! So far I have received over 800 orders for kits! Not only did I clean out my stash, but I had to find many more feedsacks to fill those orders.

Today we are fortunate enough to have reproduction feedsacks if you can't find the real thing. Or, you can substitute any special fabrics. It would be cute in all novelties, or made up in baby prints for a darling baby quilt. Don't let the lack of vintage feedsacks deter you from making this sweet quilt.

Our frugal grandmothers would never throw away good fabric. Follow their example and use the squares you have leftover from making this quilt to make the doll quilt shown on page 96.

Fabric Requirements

▶ 48—6" vintage or reproduction feedsack squares or other fabrics
▶ Green solid: 1⅓ yd.

Assembly Directions

Step 1. Join six 4" feedsack squares with seven green sashing strips to make a row.

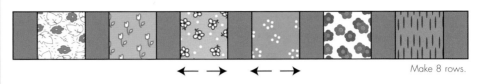

Make 8 rows.

Step 2. Join seven 2" feedsack squares and six sashing strips to make a sashing row.

Make 9 rows.

Step 3. Join the rows of feedsack squares and the rows of sashing, matching and pinning at seam intersections. Press the seams toward the sashing rows.

Border Assembly

Step 1. Join the 2" x 6" strips of feedsack along the long edges in pairs. Press the seam to one side.

Step 2. Cut each of the feedsack units into three 2" x 3½" units.

Step 3. Join 10 units and one square to make the top border. Repeat for the bottom border.

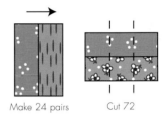

Make 24 pairs   Cut 72

Top/bottom border

Tip: *DO NOT press these borders until after they are sewn on. It will be easier to determine which way to press the seams after they have been sewn on, and you eliminate the danger of stretching the pieced border while pressing.*

Cutting Directions

From each of the 48—6" squares cut (layer and cut two at a time):
▶1—4" square
▶1—2" x 6" strip
▶2—2" squares

From green solid cut:
▶6—4" strips

From these strips cut
110—2" x 4" rectangles for sashings

Also from green solid cut and set aside:
▶4—2" strips for outside border
▶5—2¼" strips for binding

Step 4. Sew the pieced borders to the top and bottom of the quilt. Note that only the end squares and the square in the center of the border will match up with the seams in the center of the quilt top.

 Tip: *If the border doesn't fit properly, you can make slight adjustments to several seams in the border.*

Press the border seams all one direction, unless alternating with another seam. Press the border seam towards the quilt center.

Step 5. Join 15 units to make the side border. Make two. (Do not press until after sewing.) Sew to the sides of the quilt and press towards the quilt center.

 Tip: *Save leftover pieces to make the doll quilt on page 96.*

Step 6. Trim two of the 2" wide green solid borders the width of the quilt. Piece, then trim two borders the length of the quilt. Set aside. Sew the first two borders to the top and bottom of the quilt. Press the seams toward the borders just added.

Step 7. Sew 2" feedsack squares to both ends of the side borders. Sew the side borders to the quilt. Press the seams toward the borders just added.

Finishing Directions

Mark any quilting designs on the top of the quilt. Layer, baste, and bind. The quilt shown was hand-quilted with an orange peel design in the large feedsack squares, and a leaf design in the green solid sashings and borders.

Binding Directions

Before binding, hand-baste a scant ¼" from the edges to keep the layers from shifting. Piece the five green solid 2¼" binding strips together with diagonal seams pressed open. Fold the binding in half, wrong sides together, and press. Sew to the quilt with a ¼" seam. Trim the excess batting and backing and turn the binding to the back side of the quilt. Sew down by hand with matching thread.

Sign and date your vintage/new project!

For authenticity, I chose to use feedsack fabric on the back as well.

Feedsack Leaf Quilt

(58" x 78"), 20" finished blocks

Reproduction solid fabrics and vintage feedsack fabrics, hand-appliquéd by author. Hand-quilted by Pam Kienholz.

This appliquéd leaf quilt uses a traditional block in an unusual manner. A variety of feedsack prints were used for the leaves, giving a very colorful effect and showcasing the variety of prints found in the vintage feedsacks. You can make this lovely quilt using reproduction '30s prints, reproduction feedsack prints, or your own stash of vintage or new fabrics. Variety is important!

Feedsack fabric can still be found in antique stores and on eBay. I would recommend buying a bag of scraps or sets of 4" squares (you can cut two leaves from a 4" square).

Fabric Requirements

▶ Vintage white: 4¼ yd.
▶ Green solid: 1½ yd.
▶ Variety of feedsack or other prints: 124—4" squares

Suggested Tools and Supplies

▶ Easy Scallop™
▶ Freezer paper or fusible web
▶ ⅜" bias press bar
▶ Blue washout pen
▶ Roxanne's Glue Baste-It™

Cutting and Preparation Directions

Step 1. From white fabric, cut six 21½" squares (or one-half the width of the fabric). Crease them in half from both directions and from each corner, marking the center lines and diagonals.

Step 2. Make a master of your leaf block on paper. The pattern on page 119 is just one quarter of the block, placed on the diagonal.

Step 3. Lay your master copy under the white block square aligned with the center and diagonal lines. Trace the leaves onto the block with the blue washout pen. (WARNING! Ironing over the blue marks can set them permanently. We will not be ironing this block or the quilt until it is completed. Then it will first be soaked in cold water to remove the blue marks, starch, and glue.)

> **Note:** If using fusible web appliqué, DO NOT use the blue washout pen. Instead, use the master block under the fabric square to position the leaves for fusing.

Preparing the Leaves

(Make 248 print leaves, 24 green solid leaves)

Step 1. From freezer paper cut 80 or so leaves using the template on page 119. You can re-use the freezer paper templates a number of times. Or, trace 272 leaves on the paper side of fusible web and roughly cut out. (See pages 12 to 13 for more instruction on freezer paper appliqué and fusible web appliqué.)

Step 2. Iron the freezer paper (or fusible web) leaves to the wrong side of the feedsack fabrics. Cut around each leaf, adding a scant ¼" seam allowance if you are using freezer paper. For fusible web, cut out the leaves on the marked line.

Step 3. Using spray starch or a 1:1 starch/water mixture, press under the seam allowance on the freezer paper leaves. Once the leaves are prepared in this manner, remove the freezer paper template and with the tiny tip of Roxanne's Glue Baste-It, dot tiny drops of glue on the folded-under seam allowance. Starting in the center, position the first four leaves. (If using fusible web, fuse the first four leaves in position.) Appliqué in place.

Step 4. Continue with the rest of the leaves, placing them in pairs around the center. The last leaf on each branch is added after the stems are sewn on, and those last leaves are green solid.

Stems

Step 1. Cut 12—1¼" x 20" green solid strips, straight-of-grain or bias. (They can be straight-of-grain because they don't need to bend.) Sew each stem wrong sides together with a ¼" seam. Using a ⅜" bias pressing bar (or a heat-resistant ⅜" tie-down from your local auto parts store), slip the press bar into the tube and turn the seam allowance so it is on the back side of the tube, and the seam allowance isn't visible from the top. Spray with your spray starch mixture and press. Remove press bar (HOT!), and press the strip again.

Step 2. Position the stems on the diagonals, covering the tips of the leaves. Let the stems extend about ½" into the end leaf position, trim off excess. Glue-baste as before, but also thread baste in place. Appliqué in place by hand or machine. Add the green leaves at each end of the stem.

Step 3. When all the blocks have been completed, trim to 20½". Sew together in three rows of two blocks each. DO NOT PRESS as this will set the blue marker! Simply finger crease the seams.

Step 4. Using the photo of the quilt as a guide, appliqué 4 more leaves in the intersections where the blocks meet.

Borders

Step 1. Cut seven 1" green solid strips for borders, joined with diagonal seams pressed open. Make each border 10" longer than needed, but don't sew them to the quilt yet.

Step 2. Cut four 9" x 82" vintage white borders along the length of the fabric.

Step 3. Marking and matching the centers of the green and white borders, sew them together. Press the seams towards the green border.

Step 4. Measure the width of the quilt and mark two borders to this length. Matching centers and marked ends, pin, then sew to the top and bottom of the quilt, stopping ¼" from both corners and backstitching.

Step 5. Repeat this procedure on the sides of the quilt. Finger-crease the seam allowances toward the green border. Remember: we DON'T want to use an iron on the quilt yet!

Step 6. Miter each corner. (See page 14 for instructions on mitering corners.) Trim the seam allowance to ¼", finger-press to one side or open the seam.

Scalloped and Appliquéd Border

Step 1. Using Easy Scallop and the blue washout pen, mark the scalloped borders with rounded corners. To make sure the design is centered on the quilt, work from the center to the corners. I marked the top and bottom scallops at 10½" and the sides at 10". Note that the borders are cut extra generously wide to allow you to position the leaves freely. Lay the leaves on the borders until you have the spacing and arrangement that you like, then adjust the scallop size as needed. (See page 126 for using the Easy Scallop.)

Step 2. Using the tip of a stem on the block of your master template, position it under the border fabric to mark the placement of the leaves about ½" above the "V" of each scallop. (You are allowing space for the binding.) Appliqué the leaves in place as before. The green binding will provide the "vine" when the leaves are attached.

Finishing the Quilt

Step 1. Mark any quilting designs, then baste the three layers together. The quilt shown was hand-quilted around each of the leaves and stems. A daisy/leaf

design was quilted in the open areas between the blocks. A line of quilting was stitched on both sides of the narrow border. The wide leaf border was quilted in parallel lines spaced 1" apart.

Step 2. Before binding, hand or machine baste on your marked scallop line. This will keep the three layers together and prevent them from stretching. DO NOT cut on this line; keep the outside edges straight to prevent any distortion.

Binding

Cut the green solid binding 1¼" wide on the bias. Join the strips with diagonal seams pressed open. Sew the single binding to the quilt with a ¼" seam allowance. (See page 126 for instruction on binding a scalloped edge.) Trim the quilt edges ¼" from the seam line. Turn to the back side and stitch down by hand.

Washing the Quilt

To completely remove the blue marks, the glue, and the starch, soak the quilt in cold water, without detergent or presoak. You can do this in your bathtub or washing machine (but do not agitate). Let the water drain out (or spin). Repeat to make sure all the starch and glue is removed. Don't wring the quilt, but you can spin it out in the washing machine. Smooth it out on the floor or bed and allow it to lay flat while drying. Using a ceiling or box fan blowing over or above the quilt hastens the drying time.

Sign and date your masterpiece!

 Tip: *Use one of the dye magnet sheets to catch any dye that may bleed.*

Chicken Linen Quilt

69" x 93", 6" finished block

Quilt shown was machine-pieced and machine-quilted by author.

Among my grandmother's quilting scraps, templates, and orphan blocks, I found this newspaper clipping for a quilt pattern. They called it a "Beginner-Easy Scrap quilt—just two patches!" The pattern not only is easy, but also can be set a number of ways for completely different looks. See the Chicken Linen Doll Quilt page 96 for a two-color look in a Jacob's Ladder setting or the Butterfly Boogie Quilt on page 100 for yet another variation.

This pattern is ideal for using a large number of different prints, and I can just imagine my grandmother piecing it from her sewing scraps and feedsacks—sometimes called "chicken linen." Note the use of red prints throughout the quilt. Don't be afraid to mix red prints in with the reproduction pastels—with '30s prints, everything goes together! Use lots of different prints and sew them together randomly for a scrap-happy quilt.

Fabric Requirements

- Vintage white: 3⅛ yd.
- Prints: 28 fat quarters
- Red solid: 1⅓ yd.
- Print for border: 1¼ yd.

Suggested Tools

- Easy Angle™
- Shape Cut™

Block Assembly

Make 140 blocks

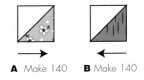

A Make 140   **B** Make 140

Step 1. Sew together all the Easy Angle triangle pairs. Press half of the triangles toward the print, half toward the white.

Step 2. Sew together all the print 2" x 21" strips with the white 2" x 21" strips. Cut each strip set into 10—2" wide units.

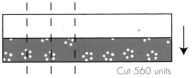

Cut 560 units

Step 3. Join different print units to make a total of 280 four-patches. Twist the center seam to open a few stitches in the center, press the seam allowances in opposite directions. See page 13.

Make 280

Step 4. Join two different triangle squares (pressed the same way) with two different four-patches. As in previous step, twist the center of the block to open a few stitches. Press the seam allowances in opposite directions. Make a total of 140 blocks.

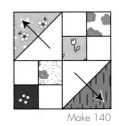

Make 140

Step 5. Arrange the blocks in rows of 10, alternating blocks with the seams pressed toward the print triangles with those that are pressed toward the white triangles. Sew the blocks together in each row, making 14 rows of 10 blocks. Press the seams all one direction, alternating the direction in every other row.

Step 6. Sew the rows together, pinning at each seam intersection. Press the rows all one direction.

Cutting Directions

From	Cut	To Yield
Vintage white	14—3½" strips	280 Easy Angle* triangles
	28—2" strips	56—2" x 21" strips for four-patches
From *each* print	2—3½" x 21"strips	10 Easy Angle* triangles
	2—2" x 21" strips	Four-patches
Red solid	8—1" strips	Inside border
	2¼" bias strips	350" bias binding
Red print	9—4½" strips	Outer border

*Layer white and print strips right sides together and cut triangle pairs. They will then be ready to chain-sew.

***Note:** If not using Easy Angle, cut 3⅞" squares, cut once on the diagonal.*

Borders

Step 1. Measure, piece, and sew the narrow red solid borders to the top and bottom of the quilt. Press toward the red border. Repeat this procedure for the sides of the quilt. (See page 14 for more instruction on adding borders.)

Step 2. Measure, piece, and sew the wide red print borders to the top and bottom of the quilt. Press toward the print border. Repeat this procedure for the sides of the quilt.

Finishing the Quilt

Mark any quilting designs, then layer, baste, and quilt. The quilt shown was machine-quilted in the ditch between each block, horizontally and vertically, and between the quilt borders. All the white areas were stippled, and a large meander was quilted in the print border.

Binding

Before binding, hand-baste a scant ¼" from the edge of the quilt to hold the layers together and to keep them from shifting. Join the red solid binding with diagonal seams pressed open. Press in half, wrong sides together. Sew to the quilt with a ¼" seam allowance. Trim the excess batting and backing and turn the binding over to the back side and stitch down by hand.

Sign and date your Chicken Linen quilt!

The Bedroom

Parasol Ladies Quilt

66¼" square, 11¾" finished blocks
Vintage and new blocks; hand-quilted by author.

This set of lovely parasol ladies blocks are from a quilt top found in an antique shop in northern Wisconsin. The lady blocks were originally set with plain white blocks, which didn't do justice to them. To enhance the lovely appliqué blocks, I reset them with double nine-patch blocks.

Quilts featuring Sunbonnet Sue (little girls with bonnets) or Colonial Ladies (ladies with hoop skirts) were very popular in the '30s era. This particular set of blocks is the best example of Colonial Ladies that I've ever seen. The ladies are so dainty; the embroidery details such as the gloves, the fringe on the parasol, and the flowers on her bonnet are just outstanding! The delightful hollyhock flowers add a special touch. Don't be afraid to appliqué these small shapes—any irregularities will only make them look more realistic! This quilt will add a sweet, feminine touch to any room.

Fabric Requirements

▶ Vintage white: 4⅛ yd.
▶ Variety of prints: 14 fat quarters
▶ Small amounts of coordinating solids for bonnets and parasols

Other Supplies

▶ Blue washout pen
▶ Fusible web or freezer paper
▶ Embroidery floss: black, white, pink, green, lavender, yellow, and blue

Parasol Ladies Blocks

Make 12

Traditional Appliqué

Using the pattern on page 67, trace the lady, parasol, and flowers onto the background square with the blue washout pen. Use the reverse pattern on page 122 to appliqué by hand or machine the lady's dress, bonnet, parasol, and flowers in place on each of the 12½" blocks (see page 12 for more instruction). Add the embroidery accents as shown on page 67. When the blocks are completed, soak in cold water to remove the blue marks and starch. Allow to dry flat. Press right side down on a towel to avoid flattening the embroidery. Trim the blocks to 11¾".

Fusible Appliqué

WARNING! If using fusible appliqué methods, (see instructions page 13), DO NOT use the blue washout pen for marking the placement. Ironing over the blue marks will set them permanently. Instead, trace the design from page 67 onto paper, and use the paper beneath the block to place the appliqué pieces accurately.

After the appliqués are fused in place, machine stitch in place with matching thread by hand or machine. Add the embroidery lines with blue washout pen at this point, then embroider the accents. When blocks are completed, soak in cold water to remove the blue markings, allow to dry flat, then press right side down on a towel to avoid flattening the embroidery. Trim the blocks to 11¾".

Embroidery

(See page 13 for embroidery stitches.)

- All the embroidery is done with two strands of floss with the exception of the fringe on the parasol, which is stitched with only one strand of black floss. Outline stitch the lady's dress, feet, gloves, and parasol with black embroidery floss.

- The parasol handle on the original blocks was satin stitched. As an alternative, you could embroider two rows of outline stitch side-by-side.

- The lady's hands, arms, and neck are outline stitched with pink floss. Her bloomers are outline stitched with floss that coordinates with her dress and are accented with French knots.

- The bonnet is embroidered with French knots in clusters of various colors to represent flowers, with green lazy daisy stitches to represent leaves.

- The appliquéd flowers are embroidered with straight stitches from the outside to the centers, with a cluster of French knots in the centers. A lighter pink floss was used for the pink flowers, and white for the yellow flowers. The stems are outline-stitched, and the leaves are lazy daisy stitches. The tips of the plants are a series of French knots in the flower colors.

Cutting Directions

From	Cut	To Yield
Vintage white	4—12½" strips	12—12½" blocks for appliqué
	10—4¼" strips	84—4¼" squares
	20—1¾" strips	79—1¾" x 10" rectangles
	7—1¾" strips	Border
Each print	4—1¾" x 21" strips	7—1¾" x 10" rectangles
	2—3" x 21" strips	9—3" squares for prairie points

Finishing the Quilt

Step 1. Using the 3" print squares cut earlier, fold in half on the diagonal. Press. Fold in half again on the diagonal. Press. Do this with each one of the 3" squares to make 120 prairie points.

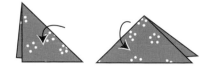

Step 2. Tuck each prairie point inside the other and machine baste (set the sewing machine at the longest stitch) 29-30 prairie points together for one side of the quilt. This border should fit one edge of the quilt exactly. If not, adjust the amount of tuck in several prairie points to make it fit. Sew the prairie point borders to the quilt top with the points turned inward and sewing a ¼" seam.

 **Note:** *The point of the triangle should come exactly to the corner of the quilt top, not extend beyond.*

Step 3. Mark any quilting designs on the quilt top. Baste the layers together and quilt. The quilt shown was hand-quilted through the diagonal on the nine-patch blocks, and curved lines in the plain squares. The parasol lady blocks were hand-quilted in the ditch around the motifs. A small scallop was quilted in the white border.

Step 4. After quilting is completed, trim the backing even with the raw edge of the quilt top. Trim the batting ¼" shorter than the quilt top. Turn the prairie points to the outside of the quilt; turn the backing under ¼" to cover the stitching line on the prairie points. Stitch down by hand. Sign and date your lovely Parasol Ladies quilt!

(Reversed pattern
for appliqué found
on page 122.)

Almost a Flower Garden Quilt

(64" x 75"), 8½" finished block
Pieced with reproduction fabrics and machine- and hand-quilted by author.

Grandmother's Flower Garden quilts are synonymous with the '30s era. Grandmother's Flower Garden and Double Wedding Ring quilts are probably the most popular and recognized quilt designs of the 20th century. However, both quilts are rather difficult to piece: Double Wedding Ring is a challenge with it's curved piecing, and Grandmother's Flower Garden is usually hand-pieced because of all the set-in seams.

I remember admiring the Grandmother's Flower Garden quilts my grandmother and great-grandmother made, and marveling at the variety of prints and the thousands of tiny stitches involved. While making some Album blocks one day, I realized they could look like flowers if arranged with prints and solids like the traditional Grandmother's Flower Garden blocks, and Voila! the Almost a Flower Garden Quilt is the result. I think you will enjoy making this quilt as much as I did. You'll find the blocks quite easy to do, and I share my secret for making those pieced borders fit every time!

Fabric Requirements

▸ Yellow solid: 4⅛ yd.
▸ Variety of prints: 20 fat quarters
▸ Variety of coordinating solids: fat eighths or scraps
▸ Screaming yellow: ¼ yd.

Suggested Tools

▸ Easy Angle™
▸ Companion Angle™

Note: *The outside triangles on the block are cut over-size so you can trim the block to size evenly when completed.*

Tip: *Put all the pieces needed for one block on a paper plate. You can do this for all 30 blocks; stack the plates and keep handy by the sewing machine. When you have a few minutes to sew a block together, all the pieces will be at your fingertips!*

Block Assembly

Make 30

Step 1. Assemble two units with a 2" print square and the yellow (larger) Companion Angle triangles along the sides.

Make 2

Step 2. Assemble two units with the 2" x 5" print rectangle and the yellow (larger) Companion Angle triangles along the sides.

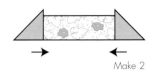

Make 2

Step 3. Assemble two units with two 2" x 3½" print rectangles, one coordinating solid 2" square, and the yellow (larger) Companion Angle triangles along the sides.

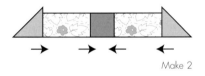

Make 2

Step 4. Assemble one unit of two 2" x 3½" print rectangles, two 2" coordinating solid squares, and one screaming yellow square.

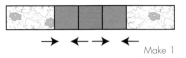

Make 1

Step 5. Join the units, matching centers and pressing as indicated. Add the corner (smaller) Easy Angle triangles last. Press.

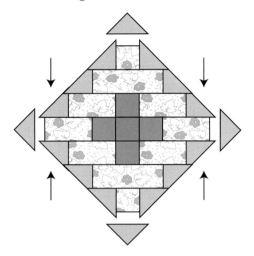

Step 6. Trim the block evenly on all four sides to measure 9", leaving at least ¼" from the corners of the print pieces. Repeat to make 30 blocks.

Cutting Directions for Blocks

From	Cut	To Yield
Yellow solid	4—2" strips	120—Easy Angle* triangles (block corners)
	18—1¾" strips	360 Companion Angle** triangles
Screaming yellow	2—2" strips	30—2" squares for flower centers
For each flower (Cut from prints)	2—2" x 21" strips	2—2" x 5" rectangles 2—2" squares 6—2" x 3½" rectangles
For each flower (cut from solids)	2" x 10" strip	4—2" squares

***Note:** *If not using Easy Angle, cut 60—2⅜" squares; cut once on the diagonal.*

***If not using Companion Angle, cut 90—3¾" squares, cut twice on the diagonal.*

Assembling the Quilt Top

Step 1. Join five blocks with four sashing strips to make a row.

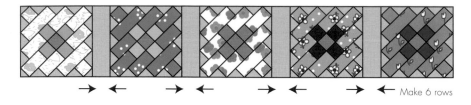

→ ← → ← → ← → ← Make 6 rows

Step 2. Sew together five sashing strips and four print squares to make the horizontal sashes.

← → ← → ← → ← → Make 5 rows

Step 3. Join the block rows and the horizontal sashing rows, matching and pinning at seam intersections. Press toward the sashing rows.

Borders

Step 1. Piece the yellow inner border strips as needed with diagonal seams pressed open. Measure the quilt top through the center, trim the borders to this measurement, then sew the borders to the top and bottom of the quilt. See page 14 for more instruction on adding borders.

Step 2. In the same manner, sew the side inner borders to the quilt.

Step 3. For the pieced border, sew the yellow (larger) Companion Angle triangles to opposite sides of the remaining squares as indicated below. Press the seams toward the square.

Step 4. For the top and bottom border, piece together 24 of the triangle/square units for each border. Remove the triangle on each end. Sew an Easy Angle (smaller) triangle to both ends. Press the seams all one direction.

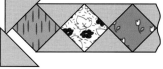

Cutting Directions for Sashing, Pieced Border and Inner and Outer Borders

From	Cut	To Yield
Yellow solid	13—2" strips	49—2" x 9" sashings
	11—1¾" strips	220 Companion Angle* triangles
	1—2" strip	16 Easy Angle** triangles
	7—3" strips	Inner border
	8—4" strips	Outer border
Variety of prints	2" x 21" strips	130—2" squares for corner stones and pieced border
	3" x 21" strips	138—3" squares for prairie points

***Note:** If not using Companion Angle, cut 55—3¾" squares. Cut twice on the diagonal.*

**If not using Easy Angle, cut four 2⅜" squares. Cut once on the diagonal.

Step 5. Trim both long edges and the ends of the pieced border straight, leaving a ¼" seam allowance from the corners of the squares.

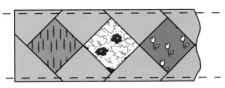

Step 6. Measure the pieced borders and the width of the quilt. If the quilt top measures more than the pieced border, trim the sides of the quilt evenly to equal the measurement of the pieced border.

> **Note:** *The inside border has been cut oversize to allow for trimming. Do not sew the pieced borders to the quilt yet!*

Step 7. For the side pieced borders, join 29 units for each border. Sew the smaller Easy Angle triangles to both ends as before. Press the seams all one direction. Trim as before.

Step 8. Measure the pieced borders and the length of the quilt. If the quilt top measures more than the pieced border, trim the top and bottom of the quilt top evenly to equal the measurement of the pieced border.

Step 9. Sew the top and bottom pieced borders to the quilt top, pressing the seams toward the inner border.

Step 10. Before sewing the side pieced borders to the quilt, open up a seam in the pieced border and insert two more triangle/square units in each pieced border. This will add the additional measurement needed to equal the length of the

quilt top with top and bottom borders added. (Trust me on this one—it works!)

Step 11. Sew the side borders to the quilt and press toward the inner border.

Step 12. Add the wider outer border in the same manner as the inner border. Press the seams toward the outer border.

Prairie Point Edging

Step 1. Using the 138—3" squares, fold once on the diagonal, press, fold on the opposite diagonal, press.

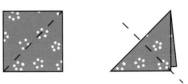

Make 138

Step 2. Baste together 32 prairie points to fit the top and bottom borders. Sew to the top and bottom of the quilt with the points facing in. The first and last prairie point should be positioned right to the raw edge.

Step 3. Repeat this procedure using 37 prairie points for each side of the quilt. Sew to the sides of the quilt.

Finishing the Quilt

Step 1. Quilt as desired. The quilt shown was hand-quilted ¼" from the seam lines in the "flowers." The yellow background area was machine-quilted with an all-over meander.

Step 2. When the quilting is completed, trim the batting even with the quilt top. Trim the backing ¼" larger than the quilt top, turn under the raw edge ¼", and hand stitch over the stitching line on the back side of the quilt.

Sign and date your lovely Flower Garden quilt!

Pineapple Swirl Quilt

Size shown: (58" x 76"), 9" finished blocks; queen size: 94" x 103"
Reproduction fabrics, machine-pieced by author and hand-quilted by Pam Kienholz.

Have you always loved the look of Pineapple quilts, but thought they were too difficult to attempt? This Pineapple quilt is EASY! EASY! EASY! All you need to do is sew Courthouse Steps blocks (similar to Log Cabin blocks) and add folded corners after each round of strips. You'll enjoy making this quilt as much as you enjoy the finished project!

Directions and fabric requirements for the larger size are given (in parentheses).

Block Assembly

Make 48(110) blocks.

Note: *The yellow and white squares are very close in size, be certain you are using the correct ones at each step in sewing the blocks.*

Step 1. Place a 2" white square on the corner of a 3½" yellow square. Mark a diagonal line on the white square and stitch from corner to corner. Trim the seam to ¼". Press. Repeat on all four corners of the yellow square.

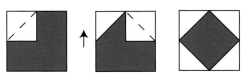

Make 48(110) block centers

Tip: *You can lightly crease the white square on the diagonal, mark a light line on the wrong side, or mark a line out from your sewing machine needle as a guide.*

Step 2. Sew different 1½" x 3½" print strips to opposite sides of the square.

Repeat for all 48(110) blocks.

Step 3. Sew different 1½" x 5½" print strips to the remaining two sides of the block. At this point the block should measure 5½" square.

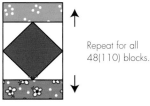

Repeat for all 48(110) blocks.

Sidebar

Fabric Requirements

► Vintage white: 3 yd. (6½ yd.)
► Screaming yellow: 3 yd. (4½ yd.)
► Assorted prints: 4½ yd. (9½ yd.) total or 20(45) fat quarters

Suggested Tools

► Shape Cut™

Cutting Directions

From	Cut	To Yield
Vintage white	10(22)—2" strips	192(440)—2" squares for centers
	24(55)—2½" strips	384(880)—2½" squares for corners
	6(14)—3" strips	70(180)—3" squares for outside corners
Screaming yellow	5(10)—3½" strips	48(110)—3½" squares for block centers
	10(20)—3" strips	122(260)—3" squares for outside corners
	7(11)—2½" strips	Borders
	2¼" bias strips	Binding to make 290"(420")
Prints	100(226)—1½" x 42" strips*	96(220)—1½" x 9½" strips
		192(440)—1½" x 7½" strips
		192(440)—1½" x 5½" strips
		96(220)—1½" x 3½" strips

*__Note:__ *If using fat quarters, cut 10—1½" x 21" strips from each print.*

Step 4. Using the 2½" white squares, position on each corner of the block. Mark and sew on the diagonal line. Trim the seam allowances to ¼". The blocks should still measure 5½" at this point.

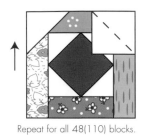

Repeat for all 48(110) blocks.

Step 5. Sew 1½" x 5½" print strips to opposite sides of the block. Sew 1½" x 7½" print strips to the remaining two sides. The blocks should measure 7½" at this point.

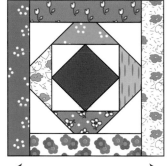

Repeat for all 48(110) blocks.

Step 6. Using the white 2½" squares, sew to each of the corners as before.

Step 7. Sew 1½" x 7½" strips to opposite sides of the blocks. Sew 1½" x 9½" strips to the remaining two sides of the blocks. At this point the blocks should measure 9½".

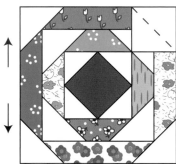

Repeat for all 48(110) blocks.

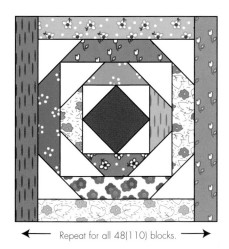

Repeat for all 48(110) blocks.

Step 8. For 24(72) of the blocks, sew 3" screaming yellow squares on opposite corners of the block, and 3" white squares on the remaining two corners.

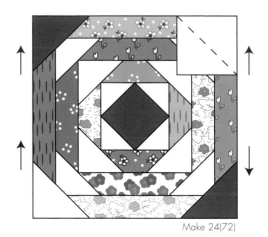

Make 24(72)

Step 9. For 22(36) of the blocks, sew 3" screaming yellow squares to three of the corners, and a white 3" square to the remaining corner of the block.

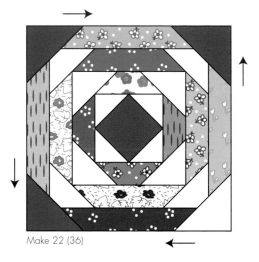

Make 22 (36)

Step 10. For two of the blocks, sew 3" yellow squares to all four corners of the block.

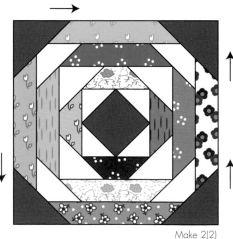

Make 2(2)

Assembling the Quilt

Step 1. For the first and last row, join five(nine) blocks with three yellow corners and one block with four yellow corners.

Step 2. For the remaining six(nine) rows, begin and end with a block with three yellow corners. The other four (eight) blocks have two white and two yellow corners.

Step 3. Lay out the rows, making sure you have all yellow corners on the outside edges. Press the row seams in alternate directions. Join the rows. Press the seams all one direction.

Borders

Join the yellow border strips with diagonal seams pressed open. Measure and cut two borders the width of the quilt. Sew to the top and bottom of the quilt. Press toward the borders. Repeat for the sides of the quilt. (See page 14 for Instruction on adding borders.)

Finishing the Quilt

Step 1. The quilt shown was hand-quilted ¼" from the seams. A cable design was quilted in the border.

Step 2. Baste a scant ¼" from the edge of the quilt to keep the layers from shifting while the binding is being attached.

Step 3. Join the 2¼" bias binding strips with diagonal seams pressed open. Align the raw edge of the binding to the edge of the quilt and sew to the quilt with a ¼" seam.

Step 4. Trim the quilt even with the binding raw edge. Turn to the back side of the quilt and stitch down by hand with matching thread. Sign and date your Pineapple Swirl!

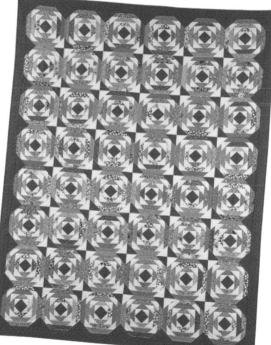

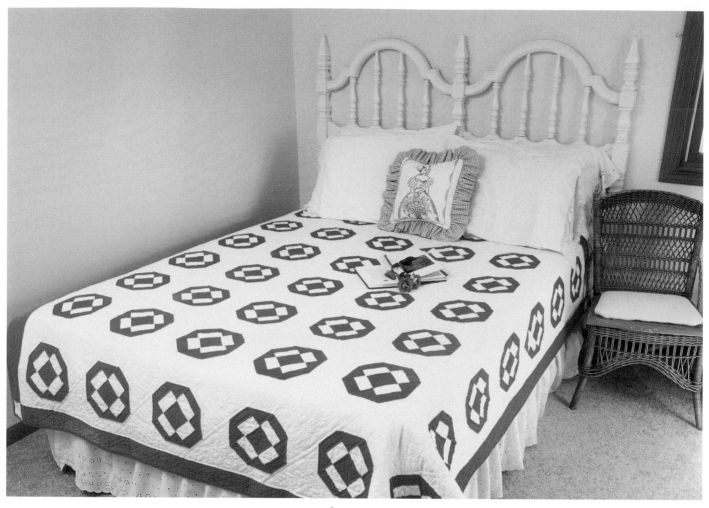

Butter & Eggs Quilt

(70" x 81"), 7½" finished block
Vintage top, hand-quilted by Pam Kienholz.

Butter and eggs—sounds like a grocery list! But in the past, butter and eggs were a housewife's source of income. She raised chickens for eggs and meat for her family, but the extra eggs and chickens were sold to supplement the family income. Most families also had a few cows, and while it was difficult to transport and sell the milk, the cream could be made into butter, which could readily be transported and sold along with fresh eggs whenever the family went to town.

Butter and egg money could also be stretched to buy fabric for new clothes—or in this case, fabric for a lovely two-color quilt! This quilt was purchased as a vintage top and recently hand-quilted. A simple block called "Grecian Designs" by Ladies Art Company, and "Greek Square" by Nancy Cabot was set on point with plain white alternate squares. The use of "screaming yellow" with white makes a dramatic statement. Notice, this quilt has a few interesting variations in some of the blocks. The Amish would call those blocks "humility blocks" (because only God is perfect), but some of us would call those mistakes! I considered fixing those blocks, but decided to leave them just as the original maker pieced made them. They are part of its charm, part of its story.

Pam discovered while quilting it, that this was a kit quilt. Typical kit quilts are appliquéd, but this is a pieced example. The shapes of all of the pieces were stamped on the two fabrics—one still had to hand cut all the pieces.

Perhaps if you are frugal with your grocery money, you too can make this quilt!

Fabric Requirements

▶ Vintage white: 4⅛ yd.
▶ Screaming yellow solid: 3½ yd.

Suggested Tools

▶ Easy Angle™
▶ Flip-n-Set™
▶ Shape Cut™

Make 42

Block Assembly

Make 42 blocks.

Step 1. Assemble 168 triangle-squares. Press toward the yellow triangle.

Step 2. Join the 1¾" yellow and white strips to make 13 strip sets. Press toward the yellow strip.

> **Tip:** Finger crease the seam before pressing to avoid curving the strip set.

Step 3. Cut the strip sets into 168—3" units.

> **Tip:** Use the Shape Cut to cut the strip sets into 3" units.

Step 4. Sew Step 1 triangle squares to both sides of the Step 3 units.

Step 5. Sew the Step 3 units to opposite sides of the yellow square.

Step 6. Join two Step 4 and one Step 5 unit to make a block.

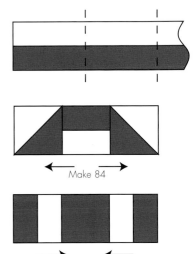

Make 84

Make 42

Cutting Directions

From	Cut	To Yield
Vintage white	7—8" strips	30—8" alternate squares
		2 more 8" squares; cut once on the diagonal for corner triangles
	5—6½" strips*	22 setting triangles cut with Flip-n-Set*
	8—3" strips**	168 Easy Angle** triangles (layer right sides together with yellow strips, then cut)
		4—3" squares for borders strip sets
	13—1¾" strips	
Screaming yellow	4—3" strips	42—3" yellow squares
	8—3" strips**	168 Easy Angle** triangles strip sets
	13—1¾" strips	
	8—3" strips	Borders
	2¼" bias strips	Binding to total 325"

*Note: If not using Flip-n-Set, cut six 12" squares. Cut twice on the diagonal to yield 24 setting triangles (you will have two extra triangles).

**If not using Easy Angle, cut 84—3⅜" squares. Cut once on the diagonal to make 168 triangles.

Quilt Assembly

Step 1. Lay out the blocks in diagonal rows, alternating pieced blocks with plain white blocks. Add the setting triangles along the edges. Join the blocks in diagonal rows, pressing the seams toward the plain blocks.

> **Note:** The setting triangles are larger than needed.

Step 2. Sew the rows together, pinning and matching seam intersections. Press the seams all one direction. Add the four corner triangles last. Press.

Step 3. Trim the edges straight, making sure you have at least ¼" seam allowance from the corners of the blocks, and keeping the corners square.

Borders

Step 1. Measure the quilt horizontally through the center, then piece and cut two yellow borders to this length. Before sewing these on, measure, piece, and cut two borders the length of the sides of the quilt. Sew the borders to the top and bottom of the quilt. Press the seams toward the borders. (See page 14 for more instruction on adding borders.)

Step 2. Sew the white corner squares to both ends of the yellow side borders. Sew to the sides of the quilt. Press the seams towards the borders.

Finishing the Quilt

Layer, baste, and quilt. An airy feather wreath was quilted in the white plain squares. The pieced blocks were quilted with a circular design in the center square, and stitched ¼" from the seam lines in the rectangles and triangles. A cable design was quilted in the border.

Binding

Step 1. Before binding, hand baste a scant ¼" from the edge of the quilt to keep the layers from stretching or shifting while the binding is attached.

Step 2. Bind with double yellow bias binding sewn on with a ¼" seam. (See page 15 for more instruction on binding.)

Step 3. Trim excess batting and backing; turn the binding to the back side and stitch down by hand with matching thread.
Sign and date your special quilt!

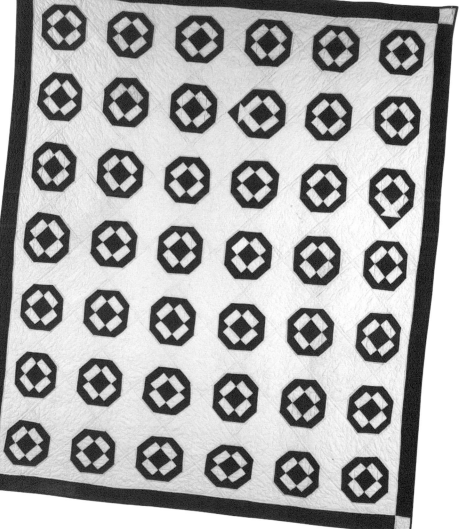

Trip Around the World Pillow

(18" square)
Machine-pieced and machine-quilted by author.

Afraid to tackle the larger Trip Around the World quilt (page 104), and would like to try something smaller? This project is for you. It uses fewer colors but is assembled in the same manner as the large one. This pillow has a bound edge, just like a quilt. It gives the appearance of a corded edge but is much easier to do. Give this pillow a try—it goes together so quickly!

Assembly Directions

Step 1. Sew together three strip sets of yellow solid and yellow print. Press. Cut these into 32—1½" units.

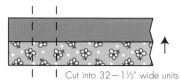

Cut into 32—1½" wide units

Step 2. Sew together six strip sets of lavender floral and lavender print. Set aside three sets for Step 3. Press. Cut these into 32—1½" units.

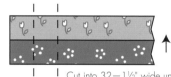

Cut into 32—1½" wide units

Step 3. Sew green grid strips to the floral side of the remaining strip sets from Step 2. Press. Cut into 32—1½" units.

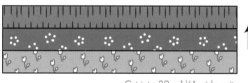

Cut into 32—1½" wide units

Step 4. Sew the yellow print end of the Step 1 units to the lavender print end of the Step 2 units. DO NOT press at this step! Make 32.

Step 5. Sew the lavender print end of the Step 3 units to the yellow solid end of the Step 4 units. DO NOT press at this step! Make 32.

Step 6. Sew the ends of the pieced units together to form 32 loops. Following the diagram given below and the piecing directions for the Trip Around the World Wall Quilt page 104, sew together the four corner units for the blocks. Cut one 1½" yellow solid square for the center of the pillow top. Assemble the horizontal and vertical center strips, and join with the four corner units to make the pillow top. Press.

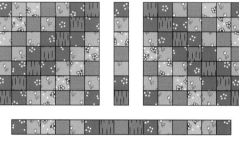

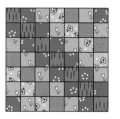

Cutting Directions

From	Cut
Yellow solid	3—1½" x 21" strips
Yellow print	3—1½" x 21" strips
Green grid	3—1½" x 21" strips
Lavender print	6—1½" x 21" strips
Lavender floral	6—1½" x 21" strips
	2—2½" x 42" strips

Borders

Cut two 2" x 42" lavender print strips. Trim two strips to the width of the pillow top. Sew to the top and bottom of the pillow. Press toward the borders. Add side borders in the same manner. Press.

Finishing the Pillow

Step 1. Cut a 19" square of muslin and batting. Layer, baste, and quilt the pillow top. The pillow shown was machine-quilted on the diagonal of each square using a wavy stitch. Parallel lines were quilted in the border. Baste a scant ¼" from the edge of the pillow top.

Step 2. Cut two pillow backs 19" x 23". Fold each in half and press so you have two rectangles measuring 19" x 11½". Overlap the folded edges to form a 19" pillow back. Baste around the edges a scant ¼" from the edge.

Step 3. With wrong sides together, pin the pillow top and backing together along the edges. Join the binding strips with diagonal seams pressed open. Fold in half, wrong sides together and press.

Step 4. Sew the binding to the pillow with a ⅜" seam, mitering the corners. Leaving a little extra batting and backing for extra fullness in the binding, trim off the excess batting and backing. (See page 15 for more instruction on binding.) Fold the binding to the back side of the pillow and stitch down by hand. Insert the 18" pillow form and your pillow is ready to use and enjoy!

Morning Glory Wreath Wall Quilt

(41" x 56"), 15" finished block
Vintage blocks set together and hand-quilted by author.

These lovely vintage Morning Glory blocks had been used for another purpose before I acquired them. They showed some wear and tear, but had never been quilted. I thought they were still lovely, so I placed them block-to-block, added a narrow lavender border and a wider yellow outer border, quilted, and then finished with a scalloped edge. This is now one of my favorite quilts, and the bright cheery colors put a smile on my face.

The blocks may have been from a kit quilt. Just as today, quilters in the past liked to buy kits—everything you need to make a project in one bag. Typical of kit quilts from the 1920s to 1950s is the use of solid color appliqués combined with wonderful professional designs. The designs were stamped on colored or white fabric and coded, so you would know where the appliquéd pieces should be placed. Often the quilting designs were marked with tiny blue dots. It was a "paint-by-number" quilt kit! You are fortunate if you own one of these beauties, but if not, you can make this lovely wall-hanging that is reminiscent of a kit quilt.

Appliqué Blocks

Make 6 blocks

Step 1. From the yellow solid, cut six 16" blocks.

Step 2. From green solid cut eight 1" x 30" bias strips for Morning Glory wreaths and stems. Fold wrong sides together, sew a ¼" seam. Trim the seam to a scant ¼", and turn the seam so that it is hidden under the bias strip (a ¼" bias press bar is helpful here). Press. Prepare eight 30" long bias strips in this manner.

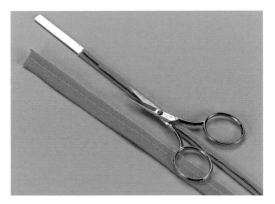

Step 3. Using the freezer paper or fusible web technique (see pages 12 to 13 for more instruction), cut and prepare the appliqué leaf and flower shapes (templates on pages 120 and 121).

Step 4. Cut 36 leaves and 18 calyxes from green solid. From each of the dark blue, pink, and lavender solids, cut six flower base shapes from each color. From the light blue, light pink, and light lavender solids, cut six flower tops from each color.

Step 5. Reversing the design, make a master template of the block from the pattern on pages 120 and 121 Darken the lines or use a light box to help you position the shapes on the yellow squares. Baste (or glue baste) the vine in place first, tucking the branches (cut from the two extra bias strips) under in the appropriate places. Hide the beginning and end under one of the flowers or leaves. Stitch down by hand or machine.

Step 6. Arrange the leaves in place over the stems and baste down, tucking the remaining stems under the leaves. Appliqué in place. Add the dark flower bases next, then cover the bases with the green calyx and the tops of the flowers with the lighter colored flower pieces. Appliqué in place.

Assembling the Quilt

Step 1. Trim the blocks to 15½" square. Sew them together in three pairs. Sew the pairs together to make the quilt center. Press the seams all one direction.

Step 2. Cut five 1" lavender strips. Piece with diagonal seams pressed open. Measure, cut and sew two narrow lavender borders to the top and bottom of the quilt. Press toward the borders. Repeat for the side borders. (See page 14 for more instruction on adding borders.)

Step 3. Cut six 5½" yellow borders. Piece with diagonal seams pressed open. Measure, cut and sew two yellow borders to the top and bottom of the quilt. Press toward the borders. Repeat for the side borders. (You may choose to miter these corners instead. See page 14 for instruction on mitering corners.)

Finishing the Quilt

Step 1. Mark the quilting designs on the quilt top.

Step 2. Cut backing and batting at least 4" larger than the quilt top. Layer, baste, and bind.

Step 3. Quilt as desired. The quilt shown was hand-quilted in a 1" grid in the quilt center, and a floral design was quilted in the yellow border. A line of quilting was stitched on both sides of the narrow lavender border.

Binding

Step 1. Mark the scalloped edge either with Easy Scallop (see directions page 126) or make your own template with approximately 6" scallops. Baste on this marked line to keep the layers from shifting.

Step 2. Cut 250" of lavender solid bias binding 1¼" wide. (See page 126 for instruction on binding a scalloped edge.) Join binding pieces with diagonal seams pressed open. Sew binding to the quilt with a ¼" seam. Trim the excess batting and backing; turn the binding to the back side and stitch down by hand with matching thread.

Sign and date your Morning Glory beauty!

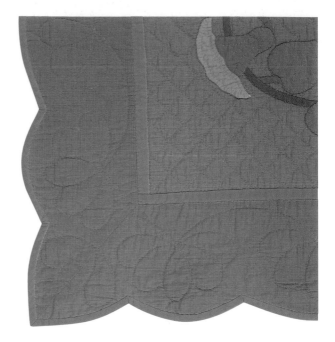

The Child's Room

Swingin' Babes Quilt

(60½" x 75½"), 7½" finished blocks
Vintage blocks set together with reproduction fabrics; hand-quilted by author.

Colonial Ladies (ladies in hoop skirts) are often seen in embroidery patterns and some quilting patterns from the '30s era. This vintage quilt top really caught my eye, however, as the ladies were pictured on swings! Just as on Sunbonnet Sue patterns and other Colonial Lady patterns, bonnets hide the faces, but having the ladies swinging is an unusual twist! I had never seen this pattern before, but after this quilt was completed, a friend in Washington sent me a picture of a quilt with identical blocks, so it must have been a published pattern.

The original quilt top was set with green solid alternate blocks, but I was unable to match the green for the border, so the alternate blocks were replaced with reproduction green fabric. This turned out to be a good choice, because when I washed the vintage green blocks, they bled terribly! Fortunately I had removed them from the quilt top before washing.

You can have fun choosing different prints for each of your ladies. The appliqué is simple, embellished with a touch of embroidery. Wouldn't this be a perfect quilt for a little girl's bedroom? (or a big girl!)

Appliqué Blocks

Make 31 blocks

Step 1. Using the design on page 123, trace the appliqué shapes on the paper side of fusible web or the dull side of freezer paper. See pages 12 to 13 for directions on fusing or appliqué. Fuse or appliqué the ladies onto the white squares.

 Note: *The design on page 123 is reversed for using fusible web or freezer paper; the design on page 89 is for placement.*

Step 2. Use the design on page 89 to draw in the embroidery details. Embroider with two strands of black floss.

Step 3. Trim the blocks evenly to measure 8".

Quilt Assembly

Step 1. The quilt is arranged with seven blocks across, nine down. Lay out the appliqué blocks alternated with the green solid blocks as shown in the picture. Sew the blocks together. Press all the seams toward the green blocks.

Step 2. Sew the rows together, matching and pinning at seam intersections. Press all the row seams one direction.

Cutting Directions

From	Cut	To Yield
Vintage white	8—8½" strips	31—8½" squares (cut oversize)
	7—2½" strips	Strip sets for borders
Green solid	7—8" strips	32—8" squares
	7—2½" strips	Strip sets for borders
	2¼" bias strips	Bias binding totaling 300"

Border

Step 1. Sew the green solid and white strips together in pairs. Press toward the green strip. Cut the strip sets into 32—4½" x 8" rectangles and eight 2½" x 4½" rectangles.

Step 2. Join seven 4½" x 8" rectangles end-to-end for the top border. Repeat for the bottom border. Sew to the top and bottom of the quilt.

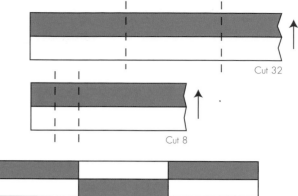

Cut 32

Cut 8

Make 2

Step 3. Join nine 4½" x 8" rectangles end-to-end for each side border. Using the 2½" x 4½" rectangles, sew four four-patches for the corners. Sew to both ends of the side borders. Sew the side borders to the quilt.

Make 2

Finishing the Quilt

Step 1. Mark, layer, and baste.

Step 2. Quilt as desired. The quilt shown was hand-quilted around the lady motifs in each block, with the suggestion of sunrays descending from an upper right hand corner. The green alternate blocks and border units were hand-quilted with a diagonal X design. The white border rectangles were quilted with a small continuous leaf design. The corner squares were quilted ¼" from the seam lines.

Binding

Step 1. Before sewing on the binding, hand-baste a scant ¼" from the edge of the quilt. This will prevent the layers from stretching or shifting while the binding is being attached.

Step 2. Join the ends of the bias binding strips with diagonal seams pressed open. Fold the binding in half, wrong sides together, and press. Sew the binding to the quilt with a ¼" seam. Trim off excess batting and backing and fold to the back side. Stitch down by hand with matching thread. (See page 15 for more instruction on binding.) Don't forget to sign and date your quilt!

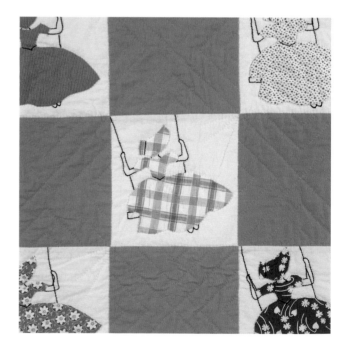

Dresser Scarf Pillow

Embroidered linens can be readily found at antique stores, flea markets, and garage sales. Even damaged linens can be used to create a decorative pillow for any room of the house.

Cut a useable square (or rectangle) from a dresser scarf or other embroidered item.

Borders could be added to make it larger or change the shape. The pillow top can be layered and quilted if desired, or used as is.

Follow the directions for making pillows (see page 29, 81 or 95), insert a pillow form, and your project is finished!

Butterfly Wreath Quilt

Size shown: (62" x 86"), 20½" finished block; full/queen-size: (86" x 86")
Reproduction fabrics, pieced, hand appliquéd, and hand-quilted by author.

A book on '30s quilts would not be complete without a butterfly quilt. Butterflies were a symbol of hope during the dark days of the Great Depression and the two World Wars; a symbol that better times would come. There are literally hundreds of butterfly designs; when a pattern wasn't available, women simply drew their own! And, just as there are many Butterfly designs, there are also many ways to set the butterflies. I saw this setting, with the butterflies arranged in a wreath, on an antique quilt. My daughter, Rachel, designed the lovely three-part butterflies for me to stitch. The Garden Maze setting frames and complements the large butterfly blocks, with the wide white scalloped border adding the finishing touch. With the addition of three more blocks you would have a full/queen-size quilt. (See numbers in parentheses for larger size.)

Fabric Requirements

▶ Vintage white: 5 yd. (6⅓ yd.)
▶ Blue solid: 2 yd. (2⅓ yd.)
▶ Variety of prints: scraps or fat eighths
▶ Variety of solids: scraps or fat eighths

Suggested Tools and Supplies

▶ Easy Scallop™
▶ Freezer paper or fusible web
▶ Black embroidery floss
▶ Blue washout pen

Block Assembly

Make 6 (9) blocks

Step 1. Using the template for the butterfly on page 124, make a master block on a large square of paper. To do this, crease the large paper square on both diagonals. Trace the butterflies, which are centered on the diagonals, having the wing tips touch. Crease each of the 22" fabric squares from both directions on the diagonal. Center a fabric square over the master block, and with the blue washout pen, trace the butterfly shapes.

Note: *If using fusible web, just use the master for placement.*

Note: *The white squares are cut 1" larger, and will be trimmed to size later.*

Step 2. Using the butterfly template on page 124, trace the upper and lower wings and body onto the dull side of freezer paper or the paper side of fusible web. See pages 12 to 13 for more instructions on hand appliqué or fusing. Complete the appliqué on six(nine) blocks. Using the master block, lightly trace the antennas. Embroider with two strands of black embroidery floss.

Step 3. After completing the blocks, if you have used the blue washout pen, soak the blocks in cold water. Lay flat to dry; press. Trim the blocks to 21" square. To do this, using your long ruler, trim just the edge of one side. Then, align the bottom (short) edge of the ruler with the trimmed edge, and trim the adjacent side. This will keep the corners at 90 degree angles. Continue in this manner around the block. Now that the block is square, measure, then trim evenly to 21" square.

Trimmed edge

Sashing

Step 1. Sew together nine(13) strip sets of blue/white/blue. Cut into 17(24)— 3½" x 21" sashes.

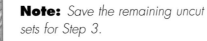

Make 9(13)

Note: *Save the remaining uncut sets for Step 3.*

Cutting Directions

From	Cut	To Yield
Vintage white	3(5)—22" strips	6(9)—22" squares*
	11(17)—1½" strips	Pieced sashing
	2—6½" x 87" strips	For borders
	2—6½" x 52"(75") strips	For borders
Blue solid	19(28)—1½" strips	Pieced sashing
	1¼" bias strips	Binding to total 370"(420")

These squares can be cut at half the width of your fabric.

Step 2. Sew the two(four) remaining white 1½" strips to both sides of one(two) blue 1½" strips to make one(two) strip sets of white/blue/white.

Step 3. Cut the remaining half(full) strip set of blue/white/blue (from Step 1) and the one(two) white/blue/white strip sets made in Step 2 into 1½" wide segments.

Step 4. Sew the units from Step 3 into nine-patches.

Step 5. Sew a sash between 2(3) butterfly blocks. Add sashes to the right and left side of the block row.

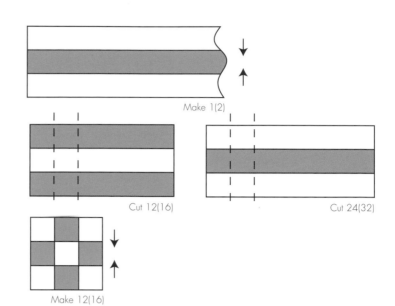

Make 1(2)

Cut 12(16)

Cut 24(32)

Make 12(16)

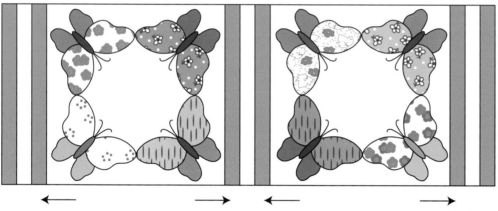

Make 3 rows

Step 6. Sew together 3(4) nine-patches and 2(3) sashes to make horizontal sashing rows.

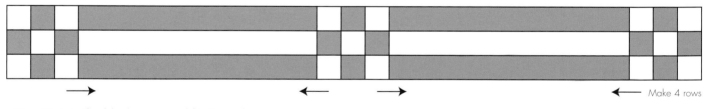

Make 4 rows

Step 7. Join the block rows and horizontal sashing rows. Press toward the sashing.

Borders

Step 1. Measure the quilt top, then trim the 6½" x 52"(75") borders the width of the quilt. Sew to the top and bottom of the quilt. Press toward the borders. (See page 14 for more instruction on borders.)

Step 2. Measure the quilt top, then trim the 6½" x 87" borders to the length of the quilt, including the top and bottom borders. Sew to the sides of the quilt. Press toward the borders.

Finishing the Quilt

Step 1. Mark any quilting designs on the quilt top.

Step 2. Layer, baste, and quilt. The quilt shown has a pretty design hand-quilted in the center of the butterfly wreath, with cross-hatching quilted around the outside of the butterflies. The butterflies, pieced sashing, and nine-patch cornerstones were quilted in the ditch. The outside border was quilted in parallel lines 1" apart.

Binding

Step 1. Using Easy Scallop (see directions page 126) set at 7¾", mark scallops on all the borders, rounding the corners. Mark from the corners to the center, adjusting the center scallop as needed. Baste, but do not cut along that edge until the binding has been attached.

Step 2. Join the blue solid 1¼" bias binding strips with diagonal seams pressed open. Sew the binding to the quilt with a ¼" seam. (For more instruction on binding a scalloped edge, see page 126.) Trim the excess batting and backing; turn the binding to the back side of the quilt and stitch down by hand with matching thread.
Sign and date your lovely butterfly quilt!

Parasol Lady Pillow

(14" square)

Vintage block made into pillow and hand-quilted by author.

This dainty parasol lady pillow will add a lovely decorative touch to any room.

Pillow Top Directions

Step 1. Cut one 12½" and one 16" square of white. Set aside the 16" square for lining. Fuse (if using fusible webbing) or transfer the appliqué design to the 12½" white square following the directions for Parasol Lady on page 63. Appliqué, embroider, and remove any markings; press. Trim block to 11¾".

Step 2. From blue print, cut two 2" strips for borders. Sew borders to all four sides of the block. (See page 14 for instruction on adding borders.)

Step 3. Layer the quilt block, the batting, and the lining and baste together. The pillow shown was hand-quilted around the lady and a grid was quilted in the background. A simple cable was quilted in the border.

Ruffle Directions

Step 1. From blue print, cut four 7" strips for ruffle. Join the ruffle strips with diagonal seams pressed open. (See page 16 for sewing diagonal seams.) Make a continuous ruffle. Fold in half, wrong sides together, and press.

Step 2. Mark the quarter points on the ruffle with safety pins. Gather (use a small zigzag over a heavy thread) the ruffle ¼" from the raw edges. Pull gathering stitches until the ruffle fits the pillow top, positioning the safety pins at each corner. At this point the ruffle should be facing in. Baste the ruffle in place.

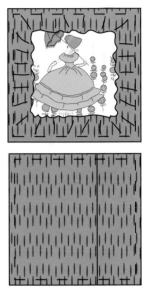

Finishing the Pillow

Step 1. Cut two blue print pillow backs measuring 15" x 20". Fold each of the pillow backs in half so each measures 10" x 15". Overlap the folded edges to make a pillow back that is 15" square. Baste around the edge to hold the two pieces together.

Note: *The pillow back is slightly larger than needed to make it easier to match up to the front.*

Step 2. Layer the pillow top and ruffle right sides together with the pillow back. Stitch a ⅜" seam around the pillow, rounding the corners for a nicer finished look. Trim the corner seams off at an angle to reduce bulk.

Step 3. Using the opening in the pillow back, turn the pillow right-side out and fluff out the ruffle. The pillow is finished; tuck in a 14" pillow form and enjoy!

Fabric Requirements

▶ Vintage white: ½ yd.
▶ Blue print: 1⅜ yd.
▶ Small amounts of prints and solids for appliqué

Additional Requirements

▶ 16" square of batting
▶ Embroidery floss
▶ Blue washout pen for transfer (optional)
▶ Freezer paper or fusible web
▶ 14" square pillow form

Chicken Linen Doll Quilt

(18" x 24"), 6" finished block
Vintage quilt blocks set together and hand-quilted by author.

When people are on vacation or travel to an event, they often purchase souvenirs to commemorate that trip or event. My "souvenirs" are often a set of vintage blocks, a vintage quilt top, or even fabric. Later, when I make or finish the quilt, I have the special memories from that trip associated with the quilt.

I found this set of vintage blocks at a quilt show in Lancaster, Pennsylvania. The set was actually much larger, but 12 blocks were all that were affordable at the time. Who says a quilt needs to fit a bed? Quilts can be any size, and the small size and sweet print of this set of blocks was ideal for a doll-size quilt. It was enjoyable putting together this small project and quilting it by hand. Consider taking home fabric or vintage quilt blocks as souvenirs on your next trip!

Tip: *Often a girl's first piecing project was to make a quilt for her doll. Being inexperienced, the quilt would not be "perfect." To make a doll quilt appear more authentic, cut, sew, and quilt more casually than usual. The points don't need to match exactly and the stitching can be large and irregular. The little irregularities can add charm to this small beauty.*

Block Assembly

Make 12 blocks

Refer to page 59 for instructions on assembling the units and the blocks, but for this quilt, make all the units the same instead of scrappy. Note the orientation of the triangle squares.

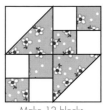

Make 12 blocks.

Quilt Assembly

Assemble the quilt in four rows of three blocks each. Press seam allowances in alternate rows in opposite directions. Join the rows. Press the seams all in one direction.

Finishing the Quilt

Mark any quilting designs; layer, baste, and quilt. The quilt shown was hand-stitched ¼" from all the seam allowances.

Binding

Step 1. Before binding, hand-baste a scant ¼" from the edge of the quilt to prevent the layers from shifting.

Step 2. Join the 2¼" binding strips with diagonal seams pressed open. Fold the binding in half, wrong sides together, and press. Sew the binding to the quilt with a ¼" seam.

Step 3. Trim the excess batting and backing and stitch the binding down by hand on the back side with matching thread. (See page 15 for more instruction on binding.) Sign and date your precious doll quilt!

Cutting Directions

From	Cut	To Yield
Vintage white	2—3½" strips	24 Easy Angle triangles*
	3—2" strips	Strip sets
Red check/print	2—3½" strips	24 Easy Angle triangles*
	3—2" strips	Strip sets
	3—2¼" strips	Binding

*Layer the white and red check/print right sides together and cut Easy Angle triangles. They will then be ready to chain sew.

Note: *If not using Easy Angle, cut 12—3⅞" squares, cut once on the diagonal.*

Fabric Requirements

▶ Vintage white: ½ yd.
▶ Red check or print: ⅔ yd.

Suggested Tools

▶ Easy Angle™
▶ Shape Cut™

Pincushion

Often in antique stores you will find the colorful pottery planters from the '30s, '40s, and '50s. Usually they are in the shape of a cute animal, but not always. Since I don't have a green thumb, I took some of the planters I've collected and made them into pincushions—something useful as well as decorative!

Materials Needed

▶ planter
▶ 6" square of fabric
▶ stuffing

Pincushion Assembly

The size of the opening varies on the planters, but a 6" square of fabric will be sufficient for most.

Step 1. Run a line of gathering stitches in a circle around the outside of the 6" square. Pull up to make a pouch.

Step 2. Stuff with polyester or wool stuffing (remnants of batting can be pulled apart and used for this purpose). Stuff tightly, pull the gathering thread tightly and fasten.

Step 3. Before inserting the pincushion, use more batting or stuffing to partially fill up the base of the planter. If you wish to weight it, add pebbles, rice or sand. This will prevent the pincushion from being pushed too far into the planter.

Step 4. Insert the pincushion, then add some colorful pins to complete the look. Instant decorating!

The Nursery

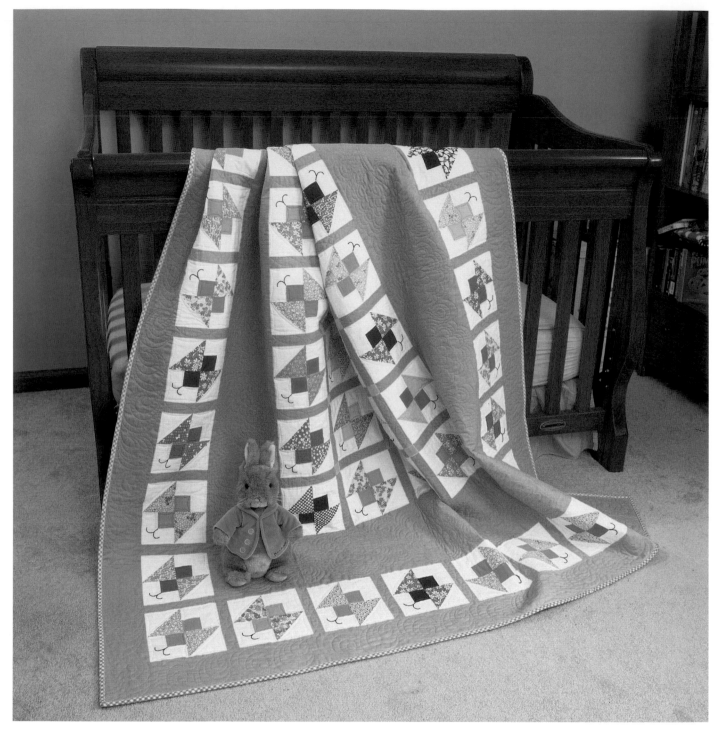

Butterfly Boogie Quilt

(62" x 76"), 6" finished block
Reproduction fabrics, pieced by author and machine-quilted by Barbara Simons of Lonestar Quilting.

While writing the pattern for Chicken Linen Doll Quilt (page 96), I suddenly saw butterflies in the design. With a slight change to the basic block, a butterfly block was created. When arranging the blocks in your quilt, you can decide which way to orient the butterflies. In this quilt, some of the butterflies will be right side up no matter where the viewer is. Antennas were added with embroidery.

Fabric Requirements

- Vintage white: 1⅔ yd.
- Vintage golden glow: 2¾ yd.
- Variety of solids: ⅛ yd. or scraps
- Light blue solid: ⅛ yd. or scraps
- Variety of prints: ⅛ yd. or scraps
- Blue plaid: 1 yd.

Suggested Tools and Supplies

- Easy Angle™
- Shape Cut™
- Black embroidery floss

Block Assembly

Make 56 blocks

Step 1. Assemble all of the triangle squares.

Step 2. Sew together the 2" white squares with the 2" solid color squares. Add a white rectangle to one side of the unit.

Step 3. Sew two matching triangle squares and two matching solid/white units together to form a four-patch.

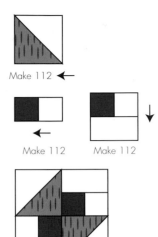

Make 112 ←

Make 112 ←   Make 112 ↓

Make 56

 Tip: *Open the center of the four-patch as shown on page 13.*

Quilt Assembly

Step 1. Lay out the butterfly blocks in six rows of four butterflies, orienting the blocks as shown, or in your own arrangement. Sew sashing strips between the blocks in each row. Press.

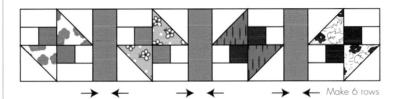

→ ←   → ←   → ← Make 6 rows

Cutting Directions

From	Cut	To Yield
Vintage white	6—2" strips	112—2" squares
	6—3½" strips	112—2" x 3½" rectangles
	6—3½" strips	112—Easy Angle* triangles
Variety of solids	2" strips	112—2" squares (cut multiples of two from each print)
Light blue solid	1—2" strip	15—2" squares for corner stones
Variety of prints	3½" strips	112 Easy Angle* triangles (cut multiples of two from each print)
Vintage golden glow	3—6½" strips	70—1½" x 6½" sashes
	5—8½" strips	Inside border
	8—4" strips	Outside border
Blue plaid	2¼" bias strips	Binding to make 300"

Layer white and print strips right sides together and cut with Easy Angle. They will then be ready to chain-sew.

Note: *If not using Easy Angle, cut 56—3⅞" squares. Cut once on the diagonal.*

Step 2. Make five horizontal sashing/cornerstone rows.

 Tip: *Only finger-press the seams in these rows. You will find it easier to fit to the butterfly rows.*

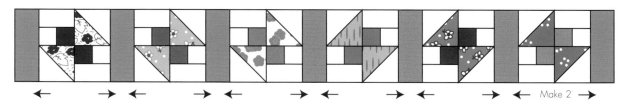

Make 5 rows

Step 3. Join the butterfly rows and horizontal sashing rows. Press toward the sashing rows.

Step 4. Measure, trim, and sew the 8½" wide yellow borders to the top and bottom of the quilt center. In the same manner, sew the 8½" side borders to the quilt. Press toward the borders just added. (See page 14 for more instruction on adding borders.)

Step 5. Sew together six butterfly blocks with seven sashes between, oriented as shown or in the direction of your choosing.

Make 2

Step 6. Sew to the top and bottom of the quilt. Press toward the yellow border.

Tip: *If the borders don't fit exactly, adjust the seams slightly in the sashing.*

Step 7. Sew together 10 butterfly blocks with nine sashes between them as in Step 5, leaving off the end sashes. Press toward the sashing strips. Sew to the sides of the quilt. Press toward the yellow borders.

Step 8. Join the 4" outside border strips with diagonal seams pressed open. Measure, trim, and sew the top and bottom borders to the quilt. Press toward the yellow borders.

Step 9. In the same manner, measure, trim, and sew the side borders to the quilt. Press toward the yellow borders.

Finishing the Quilt

Step 1. Mark the antennas on each butterfly. Embroider with two stands of black embroidery floss. See page 103 for pattern for antennas.

Step 2. Mark any quilting designs before layering. Layer, baste, and quilt. The quilt shown was machine-quilted in wavy lines with varigated thread in the butterfly wings. A diamond/oval design was quilted in the sashing, an all-over floral pattern quilted in the wide yellow border, and a swirl design quilted in the narrow yellow border.

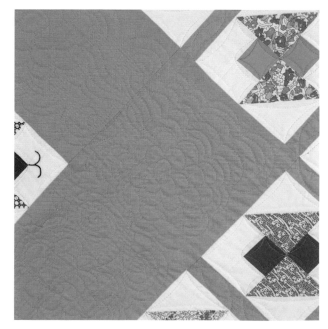

Binding

Step 1. Before binding, hand-baste a scant ¼" from the edge of the quilt to keep the layers together and prevent them from shifting.

Step 2. Prepare the binding (see page 15 for more instruction on binding). Sew the binding to the quilt with a ¼" seam. Trim the excess batting and backing; turn the binding to the back side of the quilt and stitch down with matching thread by hand. Sign and date your lovely butterfly quilt!

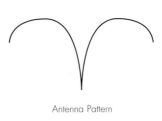

Antenna Pattern

Trip Around the World Wall Quilt

(39" square), 1" finished squares
Reproduction fabrics, machine-pieced and machine- and hand-quilted by author.

Have you always admired the Trip Around the World quilts, but were too intimidated to try one? All those tiny pieces (usually called Postage Stamp quilts as the pieces were the size of postage stamps)! This is the perfect size project to try out this pattern; not so large as to be overwhelming, but large enough to try out the strip-piecing technique.

There is also a pillow pattern (page 79) if you'd like to create a companion piece or just try a smaller format with fewer fabrics.

Fabric Requirements

▶ Green print: 1 yd.
  (border and binding)
▶ Fat quarters:
  3 yellow prints
  3 pink prints
  3 blue prints
  3 green prints
  3 lavender prints

Suggested Tool

▶ Shape Cut™

Cutting and Assembly Directions

Step 1. From each print, cut five 1½" x 21" strips. Sew three of the same color family (i.e., three pinks or three greens, etc) together into 5 strip sets. Cut the strip sets into 64—1½" segments of each color family.

Tip: *Place the lightest (or darkest) print in the center of the strip set, or graduate the three prints from light to dark.*

Step 2. Arrange the colored segments in the order that you'd like them to appear on your quilt, or match the picture on page 104. Sew the ends of the segments together in order, joining the ends to make a circle of 15 squares. Repeat to make 64 "rings." DON'T press at this step.

Step 3. Beginning with the strip just to the right of the middle of the quilt, open the seam between the lavender and the green segments. This is your first row. For the next row to the right, open the seam between the second and the last lavender square. This is your second row. Press the seams in one row one direction and press in the opposite direction for the other row. Sew together. DO NOT press the joining seam yet.

Step 4. Open the seam between the first and second lavender square for the third row. Press this row so the seams oppose, sew. Continue in this manner until you have a total of 15 rows. Make three more sections identical to the first section. DO NOT press any of the sections at this point.

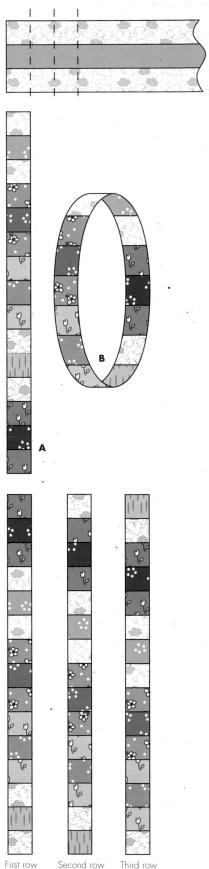

First row   Second row   Third row

Step 5. Arrange the four sections to resemble the quilt on page 107. Choose one color/print for the center square. Cut one 1½" square.

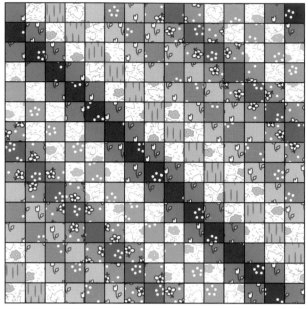

One-quarter of quilt

Step 6. Open the seam between the first and second green print on the remaining four rings. These are your horizontal and vertical center strips. Press the two top sections in the same direction and the center strip in the opposite direction. Join the three units for the top of the quilt. Repeat for the bottom half of the quilt.

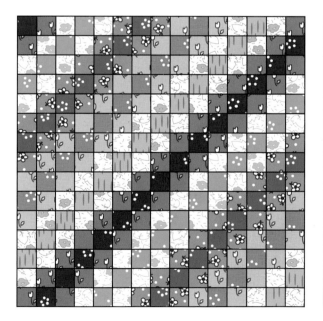

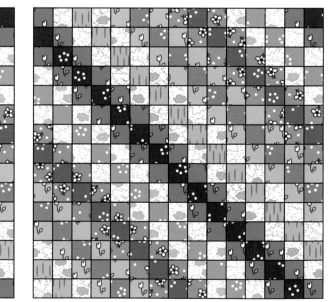

Vertical center row

Step 7. Sew the center square between the two remaining strips. Sew the horizontal center strip between the top and bottom halves of the quilt. Press the seams toward the center.

Horizontal center row

Borders

Step 1. Cut four 4½" green print outer borders.

Step 2. Measure, then trim two green print borders the width of the quilt. Sew to the top and bottom of the quilt. Press the seams toward the borders. Repeat for the sides of the quilt. (See page 14 for more instruction on borders.)

Finishing the Quilt

Cut the backing and batting 4" larger than your quilt top. Baste the layers together. The quilt shown was machine-quilted with a wavy stitch on the diagonal of each of the squares. The border was hand-quilted in a fan pattern.

Binding

Cut five 2¼" green print straight-of-grain binding strips. Join with diagonal seams pressed open. Press wrong sides together to make a double binding. Sew the binding to the quilt, mitering the corners. (See page 15 for instructions on adding binding.) Stitch the binding down by hand on the back side of the quilt with matching thread.

Sign and date your Trip!

Feedsack Doll Quilt

(17" x 20")
Pieced with vintage feedsack fabrics and hand-quilted by author.

   You can make this charming doll quilt from the leftovers of the Feedsack
Patches Quilt (page 50) or cut from an assortment of scraps.

- Feedsack 2"
squares and
2" x 3½"
pieced units
leftover from
Feedsack
Patches quilt,
OR a total of
70—2" print
squares
- Green solid:
½ yd.

Cutting Directions

From green solid, cut

- 4—2" strips.

From these strips
cut 33—2"
squares. Set
the remainder
of the strips
aside for
borders.

Assembly Directions

Step 1. Assemble 12 four-patch
squares using the 2" green
solid squares and the feedsack squares. Press.

Make 12

Step 2. Join three four-patch squares with three
2" x 3½" pieced feedsack units (or
two 2" feedsack squares sewn together) placed as sashing between the
blocks.

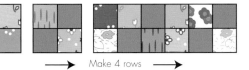
Make 4 rows

Step 3. Join three green squares and three
pieced units to make the horizontal
sashing rows. Press the seams all one
direction, so they alternate with the
block rows.

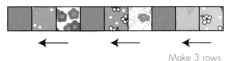
Make 3 rows

Step 4. Join the block rows and the sashing
rows, matching and pinning at each
seam intersection. Press the seams all
one direction.

Border

Step 1. Use the remaining 2" green solid strips
for borders. Trim two borders the exact
width of the quilt. Trim two borders the
exact length of the quilt and set aside.

Step 2. Sew the top and bottom borders to the
quilt, and press toward the borders.

Step 3. Sew 2" feedsack squares to both ends
of the side borders. Sew to the sides of
the quilt and press towards the borders.

Finishing the Quilt

Mark any quilting designs, then layer and
baste the quilt sandwich. The feedsack pieced
sections were quilted ¼" from the seam lines on
both edges of the zigzag. Diagonal lines were
quilted in the green squares. A leaf design was
quilted in the border.

Binding

Step 1. Before binding, hand-baste a scant ¼"
from the edge of the quilt to keep the
layers from shifting.

Step 2. Cut two 2¼" strips of green solid.
Piece with diagonal seams pressed
open. Press the binding in half, wrong
sides together. Sew the binding to the
quilt with a ¼" seam.

Step 3. Trim the excess batting and backing
and turn the binding to the back side
of the quilt. Stitch down by hand with
matching thread. (See page 15 for
more instruction on binding.) Sign and
date your sweet little quilt!

Hollyhock Garden Baby Quilt

(51" x 63½"), 3" finished block
Machine-pieced with reproduction fabrics, hand- and machine-quilted by author.

This sweet baby quilt is a variation of the Milky Way Nine-Patch (page 114). In this quilt the nine-patches are all strip-pieced; folded green corners are added to make the little nine-patches look more like flowers and leaves. I used the same zigzag setting that Milky Way uses, but added a narrow green sashing strip between each row for a completely different look. The curved edge is quite easy to do and adds a special touch to this pretty quilt.

Block Assembly

Make 81 blocks

Step 1. Assemble seven strips sets of white/pink/white.

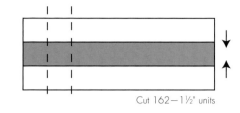

Cut 162—1½" units

Step 2. Assemble four strips sets of pink/yellow/pink.

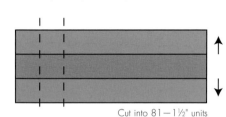

Cut into 81—1½" units

Tip: Use the Shape Cut to quickly cut the strips for the strip set, the green squares, and the units from the strip sets.

Step 3. Assemble nine-patches using the units from Steps 1 and 2. Press.

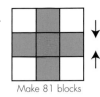

Make 81 blocks

Step 4. Place a green 1½" square on a corner of a nine-patch block. Sew on the diagonal, trim seam allowance to ¼" and press toward the green triangle. Repeat on each corner of the block.

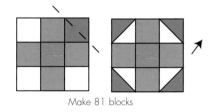

Make 81 blocks

Row Assembly

Step 1. Sew a Companion Angle (larger) triangle on opposite sides of 73 blocks as shown.

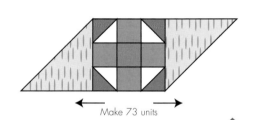

Make 73 units

Cutting Directions

From	Cut	To Yield
Vintage white	14—1½" strips	Strip sets
Pink solid	15—1½" strips	Strip sets
Yellow solid	4—1½" strips	Strip sets
Green solid	13—1½" strips	324—1½" squares
	13—1½" strips	Sashings
	1¼" bias strips	Binding to make 250"
Pink print*	13—2¾" strips	166 Companion Angle** triangles
	1—3" strip	16 Easy Angle*** triangles
	6—5½" strips	Borders

*__Note:__ If you prefer not to piece the borders, cut them first lengthwise, then cut the smaller pieces from the remaining fabric.

**If not using Companion Angle, cut 42—5¾"squares, cut twice on the diagonal.

***If not using Easy Angle, cut eight 3⅜" squares, cut once on the diagonal.

Step 2. Sew only one Companion Angle triangle to the remaining units.

Step 3. Sew together 10 units from Step 1, adding Step 2 units to both ends. Sew the Easy Angle (smaller) triangles to the ends of the row to make square corners. Make four rows.

Step 4. Sew together 11 units from Step 1. Sew together two Companion Angle triangles on a short side to make one large triangle. Sew to the ends to complete the rows. Make three rows.

Step 5. Trim the long edges of the rows even to about 5" wide. At this point the rows should be the same length, approximately 51½". Trim even if necessary.

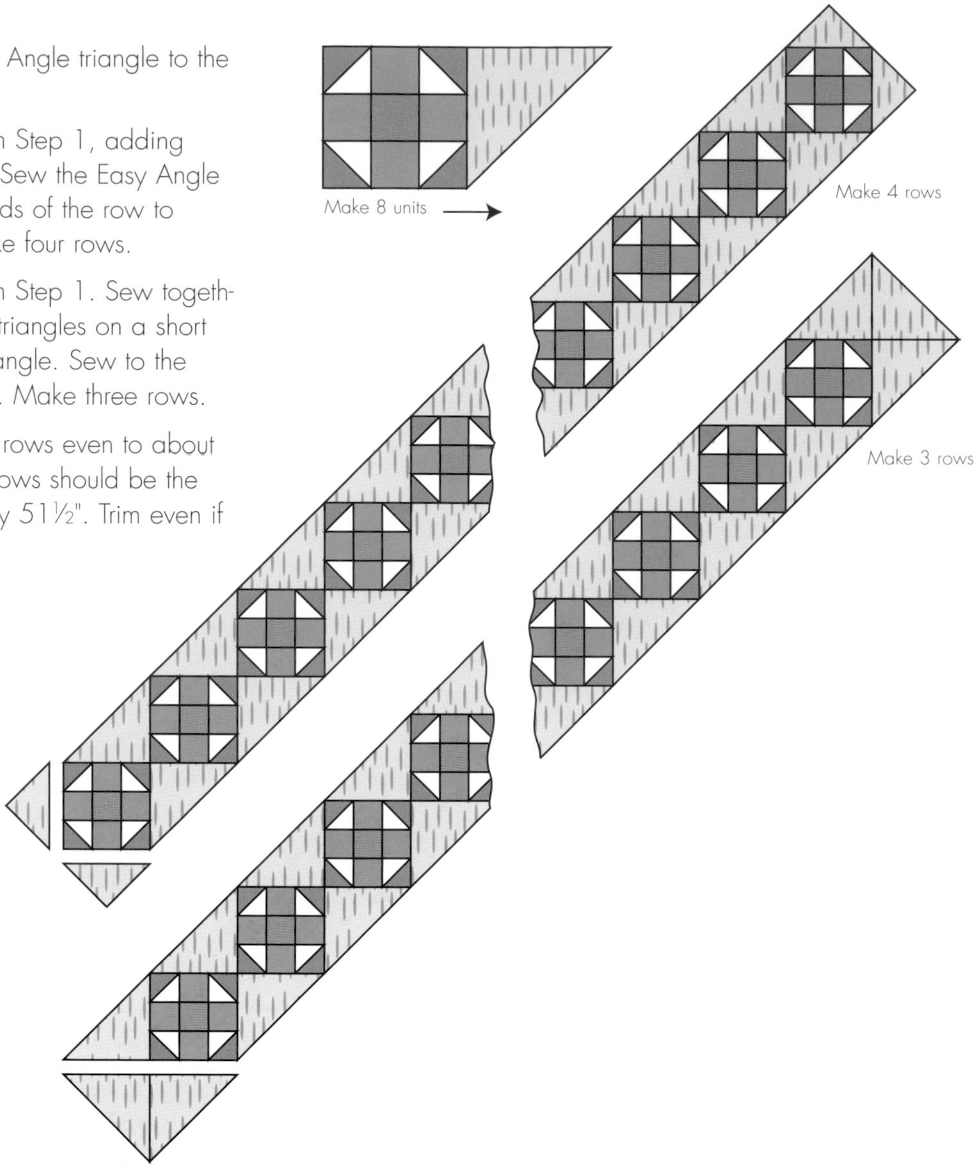

Make 8 units

Make 4 rows

Make 3 rows

Sashes and Borders

Step 1. Piece together 11—1½" green strips and cut into eight sashes the length of the pieced rows.

Step 2. Sew the green sashes between the rows and at the sides of the quilt. Press toward the sashes.

Step 3. Trim two green strips the width of the quilt. Sew to the top and bottom of the quilt.

Step 4. Trim two pink print borders to the width of the quilt. Sew to the top and bottom of the quilt. Press toward the borders. (See page 14 for more information on adding borders.)

Step 5. Measure, piece, and trim two borders the length of the quilt. Sew to the sides of the quilt. Press the seams toward the borders.

Finishing the Quilt

Step 1. Mark the scalloped border with blue washout pen before layering. (See page 126 for instructions on marking a scalloped edge.) I marked the top/bottom border with Easy Scallop set at 7¼", and inverted the tool on every other scallop to create the curved border. The sides were marked the same way with the tool set at 7".

Step 2. Layer, baste, and quilt as desired. The quilt shown was machine-quilted on both sides of the green sashing/border. A small meander was quilted in the pink print triangles, and the nine-patch was quilted in the ditch by hand. A large meander was machine-quilted in the border.

Step 3. Baste along the marked scallop line to prevent the three layers from shifting.

Step 4. Prepare the green single, bias binding. (See page 126 for binding instructions.) Sew to the quilt with a ¼" seam. Trim the excess batting and backing, turn the binding to the back side of the quilt and stitch down by hand with matching thread. Sign and date your lovely Hollyhock Garden quilt.

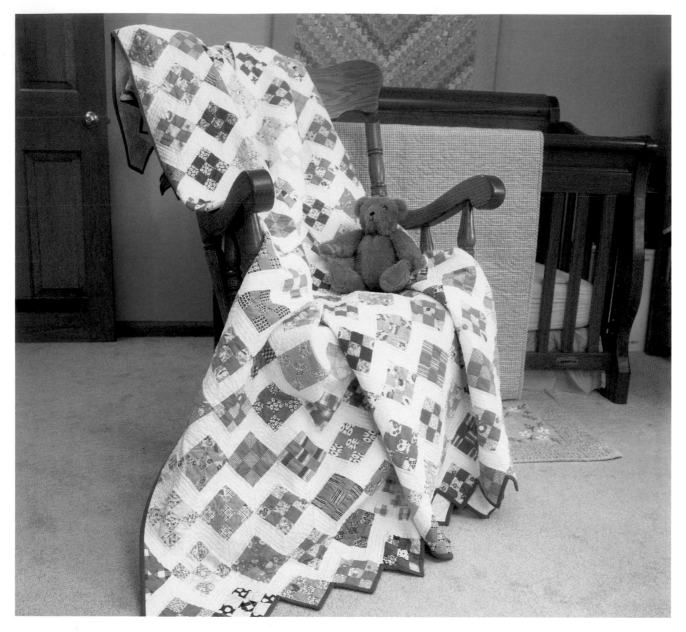

Milky Way Nine-Patch Quilt

Size shown: (81" x 89"), 3" blocks
Vintage quilt top hand-quilted by author.

This lovely vintage quilt top takes a perennial favorite, the nine-patch, and sets it in a Trip Around the World arrangement for a new twist on two old favorites! The tiny 3" nine-patches are set on point with diamonds set between them. The quilt maker who originally made this quilt top had a deep scrapbag and used lots of different prints and solids. Your blocks can be a variety of prints and solids too, or, to simplify matters, use the same print and solid for all the same color blocks.

The original maker of this quilt top chose a difficult way to piece this top together, using all set-in seams. I have made the setting much easier with the use of white triangles instead of diamonds to allow the blocks to be set together in vertical rows and no set-in seams! The original blocks measure approximately 3¼" finished, but for ease of cutting I have changed the size to 3" finished. The irregular edge naturally happens as the rows are set together. If you are concerned about quilting and binding the irregular edges, they can be trimmed straight across.

Fabric Requirements

- Vintage white: 4½ yd.
- Pink solid: ⅔ yd.
- Blue solid: ¾ yd.
- Green solid: ⅝ yd.
- Lavender solid: ½ yd.
- Yellow solid: ⅝ yd.
- Pink print (or variety of prints): ⅞ yd.
- Blue print (or variety of prints): ⅞ yd.
- Green print (or variety of prints): ⅔ yd.
- Lavender print (or variety of prints): ⅔ yd.
- Yellow print (or variety of prints): ¾ yd.
- Blue solid (binding): 1 yd.

Suggested Tools

- Companion Angle™
- Easy Angle™
- Shape Cut™

Block Assembly

Make 389 blocks

Step 1. Sew together two matching print strips and one coordinating solid strip to make a strip set. Press toward the solid. Repeat to make the following strip sets:

- 10 lavender
- 11 green
- 12 yellow
- 14 pink
- 15 blue

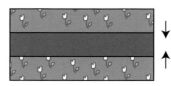

Step 2. Sew together one print strip and two coordinating solid strips to make a strip set. Press toward the solid strips. Repeat to make the following strip sets:

- 5 lavender
- 6 green
- 6 yellow
- 7 pink
- 8 blue

Step 3. Cut the strips sets into 1½" units. Sew together into 3½" nine-patches. You will need to make:

- 60 lavender blocks
- 70 green blocks
- 74 yellow blocks
- 90 pink blocks
- 95 blue blocks

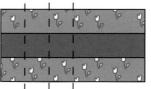

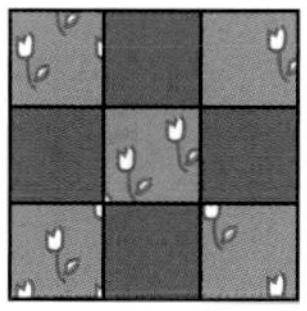

Tip: *Use the Shape Cut to quickly and accurately cut the 1½" units.*

Cutting Directions

From	Cut	To Yield
Vintage white	54—2¾" strips	702 Companion Angle* triangles
	2—3½" strips	40 Easy Angle** triangles
Lavender solid	10—1½" strips	20—1½" x 21" strips for nine-patches
Lavender prints	13—1½" strips	25—1½" x 21" strips for nine-patches
Green solid	12—1½" strips	23—1½" x 21" strips for nine-patches
Green prints	14—1½" strips	28—1½" x 21" strips for nine-patches
Yellow solid	12—1½" strips	24—1½" x 21" strips for nine-patches
Yellow prints	15—1½" strips	30—1½" x 21" strips for nine-patches
Pink solid	14—1½" strips	28—1½" x 21" strips for nine-patches
Pink prints	18—1½" strips	35—1½" x 21" strips for nine-patches
Blue solid	16—1½" strips	31—1½" x 21" strips for nine-patches
Blue prints	19—1½" strips	38—1½" x 21" strips for nine-patches
Blue solid	1¼" bias strips	Binding to equal 450"

*Note: *If not using Companion Angle, cut 176—5¾" squares, cut twice on the diagonal.*

** *If not using Easy Angle, cut 20—3⅞" squares, cut once on the diagonal.*

Row Assembly

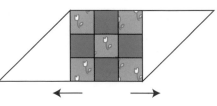

Step 1. Beginning with the center vertical row, lay out your blocks beginning with the three blue blocks in the center. Add yellow blocks at either end, then green and so on. The white triangles will be sewn on two sides of each block as shown. Press toward the triangles.

Note: *The triangles are slightly larger than needed to allow for trimming later.*

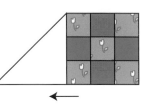

Step 2. The end blocks will only have one triangle added like this:

Step 3. Join 21 blocks in the long vertical row. Press the seams all in one direction.

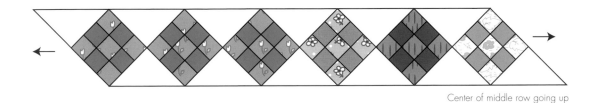

Center of middle row going up

Step 4. Lay out the blocks for the next row to the right, referring to the quilt photo for color placement. Sew the white triangles as before, but at the top and bottom, add the Easy Angle triangles instead. This will be a shorter row of 20 blocks. Repeat to make the row to the left of the center row.

Step 5. Continue sewing together vertical rows in this manner, using the quilt photo for color placement.

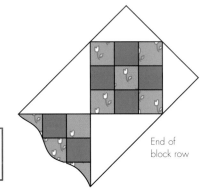

End of block row

Note: *The side rows have the white triangles added to only one side of the blocks.*

Step 6. When the rows are completed, trim the long edges even, being careful to leave a ¼" seam allowance from the points of the blocks.

Step 7. To join the rows, the point of the nine-patch on the shorter rows will match up to the center of the white triangle in the adjoining row. Match, pin, and sew the rows together.

Step 8. When the quilt top is completed, you will have zigzag rows along the side edges (refer to quilt photo), and at the top and bottom the edges will be irregular. Stay-stitch along the top and bottom edges a scant ¼" from the edge, stitching through the center of the nine-patches that extend beyond the straight edge. After the stay stitching is done, trim the top and bottom edges straight, being careful to leave a ¼" seam allowance from the points of the blocks.

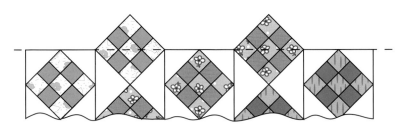

Finishing the Quilt

Layer, baste, and quilt as desired. The quilt shown was hand-quilted with horizontal and vertical lines running through the diagonal of the blocks. The white triangles were quilted ¼" from the seam allowances and twice more in the middle of the zigzag.

Binding

Step 1. Before binding, hand-baste a scant ¼" from the edge of the quilt. This will keep all the layers together and keep them from shifting while the binding is being attached.

Step 2. For ease of binding all these inside and outside corners, a single bias binding was used. Cut the binding at 1¼", join with diagonal seams pressed open. Sew the binding to the quilt with a ¼" seam. (See page 15 for more instruction on binding.) Bind the inside corners according to the instructions for binding a scalloped edge, page 126. Bind the outside corners by following the directions on page 15.

Step 3. Trim excess batting and backing. Turn the binding to the back side, turn under ¼" and stitch down by hand with matching thread. Sign and date your masterpiece!

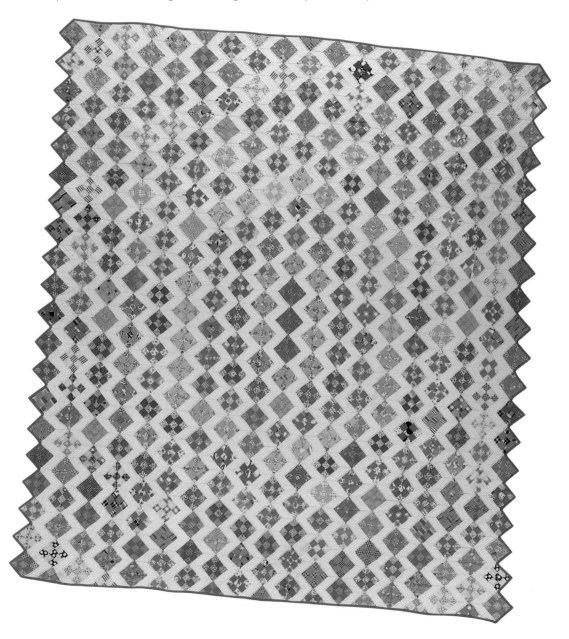

Cherry Template (Projects on pages 38, 42, 46, and 48)

(reversed for tracing)

Fan-cy Dancing Templates (Project on page 18)

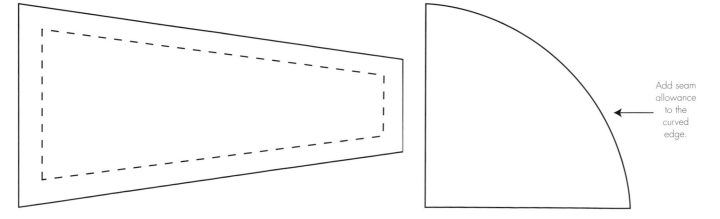

Add seam
allowance
to the
curved
edge.

Feedsack Leaf Quilt Template

(Projects on pages 22 and 54)

Morning Glory Template

(Project on page 82)

Parasol Lady Template

(Projects on pages 62 and 94)

(reversed for tracing)

Picnic Basket Template

(Project on page 38)

Swingin' Babes Template

(Project on page 86)

(reversed for tracing)

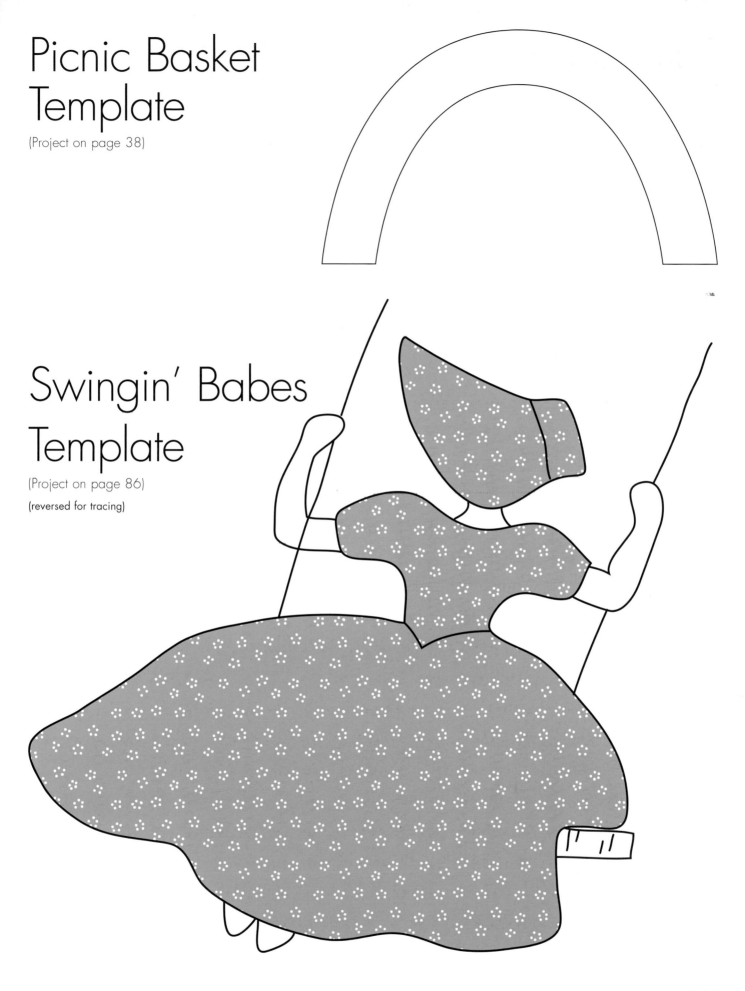

Butterfly Template

(Project on page 90)

Tool Tutorial

Easy Angle™

This tool is available in a 4½" size and a 6½" size. The larger size is recommended for the projects in this book.

To cut triangle-squares, layer the fabric strips right sides together and cut with the Easy Angle. They will then be ready to sew.

Step 1. For the first cut (after selvages have been trimmed), align the flat tip of the tool with the top of the strip, matching a line on the tool with the bottom of the strip. Cut on the diagonal edge.

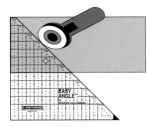

Step 2. To make the second cut, rotate the tool so the flat tip is aligned with the bottom of the strip, and a line on the tool is aligned with the top of the strip. Cut again.

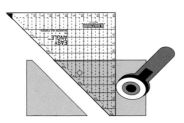

Step 3. Repeat this procedure for the rest of the triangle-squares. Chain-sew the triangle-squares on the diagonal edge. Press toward the darkest triangle and trim off dog-ears.

Companion Angle™

Companion Angle allows you to cut quarter-square triangles—triangles with the longest edge on the straight of grain. A common use for this type of triangle is the "goose" in flying geese units.

Step 1. To cut with Companion Angle, align the flat tip of the tool with the top edge of the strip. Align the bottom of the strip with a line on the tool. Cut on both sides of the tool for the first cut.

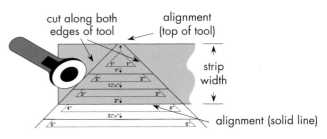

Step 2. For the second cut, rotate the tool so the flat tip is at the bottom of the strip and a line on the tool is aligned at the top of the strip. Cut again.

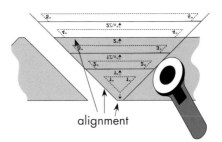

Easy Dresden™

Easy Dresden cuts many sizes of wedges for fans or Dresden Plates. The top of the wedge can be turned for a finished point (see Fan-cy Dancing Quilt page 19) or rounded with the template included in the package.

To use the tool, cut a strip the desired width. For the first cut, align the narrow end of the tool with the bottom of the strip. Cut on both sides of the tool. Rotate the tool so the narrow end is at the top of the strip. Cut again.

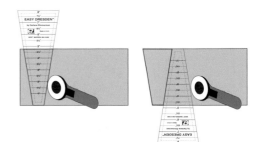

Easy Scallop™

Measuring:

Measure the length of the border. Choose the desired number of scallops. Divide the border length by that number to yield the scallop size. Round the answer to the nearest quarter inch. Set the Easy Scallop tool at that size. EX: 72" border divided by 7 scallops = 10.285. Round to 10¼". Set the tool at 10¼".

Marking:

To mark a rounded corner, begin at the very corner of the quilt and mark a full scallop. Mark from both ends toward the center, and adjust the center scallop as needed. When you mark the adjacent edge with a full scallop, the corner will automatically be rounded.

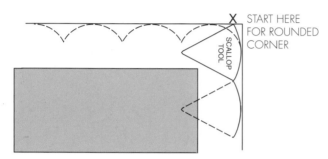

To mark a pointed corner or "ears," begin at one corner with a half scallop. Again, mark from both ends to the center, adjusting the center scallop as needed. As you mark the adjacent side with a half scallop, the "ear" will be formed.

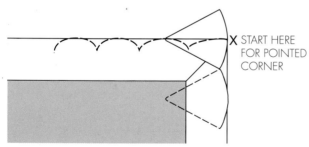

Binding:

Do not cut on marked line! Quilt, then before binding, hand-baste along the marked line to keep the layers from shifting when the binding is attached.

A bias binding is a must for binding curved edges. Cut a 1¼" single bias binding. (See page 15 for more instructions on preparing binding.)

Step 1. With raw edge of binding aligned with the marked line on your quilt, begin sewing a ¼" seam. Stitch to the base of the V, stop with the needle down, and lift the presser foot.

Step 2. Pivot the quilt and binding around the needle. Put the presser foot down and begin stitching out of the V, taking care not to stitch any pleats into the binding.

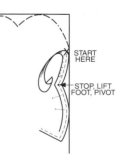

Step 3. Continue around the quilt in this manner, easing the binding around the curves and pivoting at the inside of the V.

Step 4. Trim the seam allowance an even ¼", turn to the back side and stitch down by hand with matching thread, covering the stitching line. At the V, the binding will just fold over upon itself making a little pleat.

Flip-n-Set™

Instructions:

Step 1. With the tool open, find the finished size of the blocks to be set on point and cut strips to the width indicated on the tool.

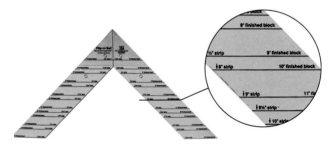

Step 2. Lay the tool on the strip with the point aligned at top of the strip and match the measurement line along the bottom of the strip. Cut on the outside edge of the tool.
Note: Flip-n-Set cuts generous size triangles to allow for trimming.

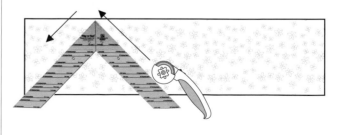

Step 3. Rotate the tool and align the point with the bottom of the strip and the edge of the tool with the edge of the fabric. Make the second cut.

Step 4. Repeat, rotating the tool and cutting to the end of the strip.

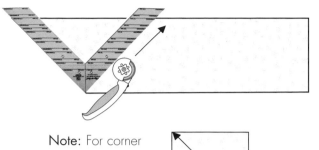

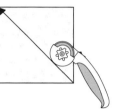

Note: For corner triangles cut two squares the size of the finished blocks. Cut each on the diagonal.

For Blocks with Sashing: Add the finished width of one sashing to the finished size of the block to determine the size of strip to cut for the setting triangles.

EXAMPLE: 12" block + 2" sashing = 14" blocks.

June Taylor Shape Cut™

To Cut Strips:

Step 1. Fold the fabric selvage to selvage.

Step 2. Fold again in the same direction.

Step 3. Lay the Shape Cut™ over the fabric, with raw edges extending slightly beyond the vertical slot marked "O" and the bottom fold of the fabric at the horizontal line marked "O".

Step 4. To square up the raw edge of the fabric, insert the blade in the "O" slot marking and cut.

Step 5. Cut subsequent strips to the desired width.

All these tools can be found at your local quilt, craft or fabric store. If you cannot find the EZ tools locally, you can call 1-800-660-0415 to order from EZ Quilting by Wrights.

Triangle Tables for Easy Angle™

Finished Size of Triangle	From	Number from Strip
½" triangles	1" strip	50
1" triangles	1½" strip	38
1½" triangles	2" strip	30
2" triangles	2½" strip	26
2½" triangles	3" strip	22
3" triangles	3½" strip	20
3½" triangles	4" strip	18
4" triangles	4½" strip	16
4½" triangles	5" strip	14
5" triangles	5½" strip	12
5½" triangles	6" strip	12
6" triangles	6½" strip	12

Triangle Tables for Companion Angle™

Finished Base of Triangle	From	Number from Strip
1" triangles	1" strip	34
2" triangles	1½" strip	23
3" triangles	2" strip	17
4" triangles	2½" strip	13
5" triangles	3" strip	12
6" triangles	3½" strip	9
7" triangles	4" strip	8
8" triangles	4½" strip	7
9" triangles	5" strip	7
10" triangles	5½" strip	5